D0290843

ELEGAIC ROMULUS

AESOP'S FABLES

An Intermediate Latin Reader

Latin Text with Running Vocabulary and Commentary

Greta Smith
Evan Hayes
and
Stephen Nimis

Elegiac Romulus *Aesop's Fables*: An Intermediate Latin Reader: Latin Text with Running Vocabulary and Commentary

First Edition

© 2017 by Evan Hayes, Stephen Nimis, and Greta Smith

All rights reserved. Subject to the exception immediately following, this book may not be reproduced, in whole or in part, in any form (beyond copying permitted by Sections 107 and 108 of the U.S. Copyright Law and except by reviewers for the public press), without written permission from the publisher. The authors have made a version of this work available (via email) under a Creative Commons Attribution-Noncommercial-Share Alike 3.0 License. The terms of the license can be accessed at www.creativecommons.org.

Accordingly, you are free to copy, alter and distribute this work under the following conditions:

1. You must attribute the work to the author (but not in a way that suggests that the author endorses your alterations to the work).

2. You may not use this work for commercial purposes.

3. If you alter, transform or build up this work, you may distribute the resulting work only under the same or similar license as this one.

ISBN-10: 1940997194

ISBN-13: 9781940997193

Published by Faenum Publishing, Ltd.

Cover Design: Evan Hayes

Fonts: Garamond

editor@faenumpublishing.com

TABLE OF CONTENTS

ACKNOWLEDGMENTS

The idea for this project grew out of work that we, the authors, did with support from Miami University's Undergraduate Summer Scholars Program, for which we thank Martha Weber and the Office of Advanced Research and Scholarship. Work on the series, of which this volume is a part, was generously funded by the Joanna Jackson Goldman Memorial Prize through the Honors Program at Miami University. We owe a great deal to Carolyn Haynes, and the 2010 Honors & Scholars Program Advisory Committee for their interest and confidence in the project.

The technical aspects of the project were made possible through the invaluable advice and support of Bill Hayes, Christopher Kuo, and Daniel Meyers. The equipment and staff of Miami University's Interactive Language Resource Center were a great help along the way. We are also indebted to the Perseus Project, especially Gregory Crane and Bridget Almas, for their technical help and resources. We also profited greatly from advice and help on the POD process from Geoffrey Steadman. All responsibility for errors, however, rests with the authors themselves.

For Tori

Fuscat et extinguit cordis caligo nitorem
Corporis: est animi solus in orbe nitor

Introduction

The aim of this book is to make the most famous medieval version of *Aesop's Fables*, the elegiac Romulus, accessible to intermediate students of Ancient Latin. The running vocabulary and grammatical commentary are meant to provide everything necessary to read each page so that readers can progress through the text, improving their knowledge of Latin while enjoying this delightful version of Aesop's Fables.

The elegiac Romulus is a great text for intermediate readers. It was used in the Middle Ages for teaching Latin grammar to intermediate students, and it is not hard to see why. The use of fables allows students to work with short but complete chunks of text at a time, and the plot lines are simple and easy to understand. These fables would already be somewhat familiar to students learning to read, providing helpful context for each selection. For such students, as for English-speaking students today, the case system of Latin substantives tends to present the greatest number of problems, particularly in verse where word position is often more free. Our author often displays mannered phrasing that seems to call attention to the need for close observation of case endings. For example, he makes frequent use of *polyptoton*, the use of the same word in different cases, which seems designed to teach the forms and cases.

The Elegiac Romulus

While fable collections had been consistently popular since approximately the 5th century BCE, when the slave Aesop was purported to have spread moral wisdom through countless pithy short stories using largely animal characters, by the thirteenth century, there is only one collection that retained popularity. The collection, which is contained in this reader, is known as the elegiac Romulus, to distinguish it from the prose versions of the collections attributed to the apocryphal Romulus. The elegiac Romulus was likely written in the late twelfth century, and was remarkably popular, as is evidenced by over 170 extant manuscripts containing some portion of this collection. These manuscripts have been dated largely from the thirteenth to fifteenth centuries, and were (and in many cases still are) located throughout Europe, with the majority being from Britain, France, and Germany. The fable collection consists largely of fables taken from classical models; however, most of these fables have been rewritten, and put into quantitative elegiac verse by the medieval author. The collection also includes a few longer fables, not found in classical sources. There are a number of possibilities for the author of this text, the leading one, put forward by Leopold Hervieux in 1884, is Gualterus Panormitanus, more commonly known as Walter of England, who was the chaplain of Henry II of England in the 12th century.

The fables of the elegiac Romulus were a part of the *Auctores Octo Morales*, a collection of works that was used in medieval Latin education. The other seven texts of the collection are as follows: the *Distichs of Cato*; *The Eclogue of Theodulus*; *Facetus*; *Floretus*; *De Contemptus Mundi*; Matthew of Vendome's *Tobias*; and Alan of Lille's *Liber Parabolarum*.[1] Each of these texts has imbedded moral lessons for their reader, and are all relatively elementary in their use of Latin. The use of the *Auctores Octo* as an educational text was widespread enough that the collection was put into print by Matthias Bonhomme of Lyon in 1538, and continued to be used as a part of education in this form. Even these print versions show evidence of significant wear, meaning that the *Auctores Octo* enjoyed popularity for well over two hundred years.[2] Early manuscript versions containing portions of the *Auctores* indicate that it was originally the Avianus fable collection, a shorter Latin verse collection from the 5th c CE, which was included in the *Auctores Octo*, but in the thirteenth century the elegiac Romulus replaced the Avianus. In his study on fables, Edward Wheatley argues that this substitution, along with the failure of the elegiac Romulus to appear alone in manuscripts before the thirteenth century, indicates that these fables may have been translated and revised from earlier versions precisely for inclusion in the grammar text.[3]

There is another fable collection attributed to Romulus that circulated in the Middle Ages, but it is in prose. This prose Romulus predates the elegiac Romulus considerably; it is speculated to have been written as early as the 6th century. The most obvious difference between the two collections is that the earlier one is a prose fable collection, while the elegiac Romulus is written in elegiac distichs. There are 98 fables in the prose Romulus, while there are only

---

[1]   In the introduction to his English translation of the entire reader (*An English Translation of Auctores Octo, A Medieval Reader*, The Edwin Mellen Press: Lewiston, New York, 1999), Ronald Pepin details the contents of each of these other works in the reader.

[2]   Pepin 2

[3]   Wheatley 55. The possibility of a thirteenth century author for the elegiac Romulus means that this author would have been educated in the same grammatical nuances of the twelfth century which the work is trying to impart upon its audience, making this one of the earliest texts written specifically for a grammar school curriculum.

60 (or up to 63, depending on the manuscript) in the elegiac Romulus. Both of the Romulus collections take the large majority of their fables from the earliest Latin translation of *Aesop's Fables* made by Phaedrus in the first century BCE. Both medieval collections revise the form and language of these fables, while keeping the same animal characters and general plots. Where the fables of the prose Romulus are in many instances very similar in wording to the fables of Phaedrus, the elegiac Romulus differs greatly, taking more influence from the collection of fables made by Avianus (also in elegiac distichs), while also reflecting the needs of its schoolboy readers.

While most modern readers are familiar with the fable genre, it is important to understand that what we define as a fable, and what the medieval reader defined as a fable is markedly different. As Wheatley argues, the fable in the Middle Ages resembles a mode of discourse or a method of communicating information far more strongly than it does a literary genre. Rather than having a set of traits that are identifiable and traceable across collections, the medieval fable instead adheres to a set of rhetorical practices including attributing the fables to Aesop, animal characters who behave as humans, and a moral application for the fable. Often, however, even these basic traits are missing; yet a fable would still be identifiable as such, especially to other medieval readers. Some fables are the simple animal stories most commonly associated with the genre, while others contain no animal characters at all, and still others mix human and animal characters rather improbably. While not as short as our modern versions, many of the fables are shorter, 8-10 line tales, with a two-line moral, but others are quite long, seeming more like a folk tale than a fable. Some fables are devoted almost entirely to moralizing, so that there is very little plot or story, but rather a moral lesson repeatedly expounded upon by a narratorial voice. Therefore, there are a number of fables in this collection that may not seem much like we would expect a fable to be, but for the medieval reader it is their location in a collection which allows all of them to be identified as fables.

One thing that is particularly notable when looking at the manuscript versions of the elegiac Romulus is that there is an incredible amount of consistency, especially given that the extant manuscripts span at least two centuries, and range in origin from Germany to Britain. The same fables are always presented in the same order (except where leaves of the manuscript had been lost), and they are almost always marked in similar ways by the scribes (similar rubrication, titling, etc.). With very little exception, the manuscript copies of the fables are neat and clearly written, but rather simple. Each new fable is marked with a larger first initial, and in many copies the color of this initial alternates between red and blue, which would have helped the reader in distinguishing between the fables. The first letters of each line are also often set aside slightly from the rest of the line, and are rubricated with a red "slash" diagonally through the letter-- this makes the lines easy to follow, and would help the reader to better find their place in the fable. The titles of the fables are in the centers of the stanzas, meaning that they can be very easily overlooked in favor of these first initials.

Careful study of the fable manuscripts makes it clear that the fables at the beginning of the collection were more commonly read and studied than the fables towards the end of the collection. In manuscripts with any amount of illustration, it is only the first twenty, sometimes even just the first twelve fables, that have marginal illustration. If the manuscript has any kind of illumination, the illuminated letters can be found only in these first fables, and even the larger first letters of the first lines of the fables are much more ornately decorated in red and blue ink in the first twelve to twenty fables. There is even greater care given to the on-page presentation of these first fables; the handwriting is generally clearer, with fewer abbreviations, and the fables are often arranged so that there are very few lines hanging over on to other pages. The titles of these fables are not forgotten, nor are any of the initials left unrubricated. In manuscripts that have scholastic commentary, the commentary is often only found in, or is much more extensive in, these first fables (with the exception of the two manuscripts that have commentary throughout).

It is also notable when reading the collection that the first twelve to twenty fables of the elegiac Romulus seem to make up a relatively coherent group. Because this was a curricular text, this would indicate that these texts would be taught first, and the student would have to devote special attention to them, not just because of the grammar they utilize, but also to learn to navigate the language of the fable genre. The inclusion of images, titles, rubricated initials, and illuminated first letters in this first group of fables all point to the importance of these fables. When looking at the fable collection as a whole, however, these first twelve to twenty fables serve not only as a guide to the reader as they work to understand the Latin grammar, but also as a guide to how the rest of the collection is to be read as a text. The first twenty fables introduce the reader to almost every animal character that appears in the entire collection (the only animal not included in these first fables that appear later in the collection are a few specific breeds of birds and a weasel). The protagonists of the first twenty fables are relatively varied, including the lamb, the mouse, various birds, an ass, and a few human characters. The animal antagonists are less varied; wolves are shown consistently to be evil, as are lions, and birds of prey such as the eagle and kite. These fables also begin rather simply, where the reader can easily see the moral lessons being taught, and there are often only two characters used in the body of the fable. As the collection progresses the fables get increasingly longer and more complex, building on the skills that are developed in these earlier fables. The patterns in the first fables illustrate the types of moral lessons that the readers are to extrapolate; many are social lessons, or instructions on what types of people ought to be trusted (or avoided as the case may be) rather than lessons on how to behave. In the most complex of fables, moral guidance is also offered in the middle of the fable, encouraging the reader to work to sort out the relationships among characters.

These features, all of which highlight the elegiac Romulus' role in the medieval classroom, combine to make this collection unique, and worthy of further study. It served as a reader to teach grammar to its medieval readers, and it can retain the same function for us today. The vocabulary is repetitive, and the grammar is straightforward, making it an excellent text for intermediate readers. The individual fables offer natural divisions, but if the text is read through from beginning to end, you will certainly note some of the patterns across fables, and develop familiarity with the animal characters and moral lessons just as the medieval reader would have. The author of the text seems to have been something of a jokester, and some passages are difficult to interpret because they are a bit of a play on words; likely these jokes were also difficult for the medieval reader as well, so at least the modern reader is in good company. Ultimately, this collection of fables taught Latin grammar to medieval readers from the late 12th century until at least the 1600s, and it is an excellent text to continue to do so today.

Versification

The verse of the collection is elegiac couplets, a form used for many kinds of classical and medieval poetry, among which are the *Distichs of Cato* and the *Fables* of Avianus. Like other classical verse forms, it consists of alternating patterns of long and short syllables. For this reason, scanning the verse can help disambiguate the cases of substantives in certain instances (the nominative and ablative singular of first declension nouns and adjectives, for example). For each elegiac couplet there is a regular dactylic hexameter followed by two dactylic hemistichs (sometimes called a "pentameter"), as follows:

$$- \smile \smile - \smile \smile - \parallel \smile \smile - \smile \smile - \smile \smile - \times$$

$$- \smile \smile - \smile \smile - \parallel - \smile \smile - \smile \smile \times$$

where "$-$" indicates a long syllable, "$\smile$" a short syllable, "$\times$" either a long or short (*anceps*) syllable, and "$\parallel$" the *caesura*, a sense pause that "cuts" a metrical foot. As is typical of classical dactylic meter, a long syllable can substitute for two short syllables, replacing a dactyl (– ⌣ ⌣) with a spondee (– –).

The Woodcuts

The woodcuts included in this text are taken from images in Heinrich Stein-howel's 1480 German edition of the fables, the first printed version of the collection. We have very few clues as to who the artist of these woodcuts was (one leading theory is Jorg Syrlin the Elder, who was famous for carving the choir stalls at the Ulm Catherdral in 1474), but these images were copied so widely that the unknown artist's illustration work has become synonymous with the early modern fable. Julien Macho of Lyons almost immediately translates the fables into French, copying the woodcuts exactly, and they are again copied by William Caxton in his English edition in 1484. A version of Caxton's text with woodcuts is available on Early English Books Online.

The Latin Text

The Latin text was taken from the Latin Library (http://www.thelatinli-brary.com/anon.nev.html), and the wording was verified against the manuscript copies of the elegiac Romulus in the British Library. The orthography has been normalized (e.g., diphthongs and palatalization) along with other minor changes. This is not a scholarly edition.

Aaron Wright (1997) published the Latin text of the elegiac Romulus, and his edition reproduces some of the medieval commentary in the margins of the pages, making for an interesting look at the medieval presentations of the fable text; Laura Gibbs also has the Latin fable text on her site, www.mythfolklore. net. Ronald Pepin's (2000) translation of the entire Auctores Octo provides the only English translation of the elegiac Romulus.

Texts and Translations

Pepin, Ronald E. *An English Translation of Auctores Octo, a Medieval Reader*. The Edwin Mellen Press, 2000.

Wright, Aaron Eugene, Pontifical Institute of Mediaeval Studies, and University of Toronto Centre for Medieval Studies. *Fabulae*. PIMS, 1997.

Gibb, Laura. "Aesop (Walter of England - Nevelet)." N.p., n.d. Web. 27 June 2016.

Other Fable Collections

Babrius. *Babrius and Phaedrus*. Cambridge, Mass.: London: Harvard University Press; W. Heinemann, 1984. Loeb Classical Library, 436.

Ellis, Robinson. *The Fables of Avianus*. BiblioBazaar, 2008. Print

Goldschmidt, A. *An Early Manuscript of the Aesop Fables of Avianus and Related Manuscripts*. Princeton, NJ, 1947. Print.

Henryson, Robert, and Denton Fox. *The Poems of Robert Henryson*. Oxford: Clarendon Press, 1981. Print.

Lenaghan, R. T, William Caxton, and Aesop. *Caxton's Aesop*. Cambridge: Harvard University Press, 1967. Print.

Lydgate, John, H N. b. 1880 MacCracken, and Merriam Sherwood. "*Isopes Fabules*." The Minor Poems of John Lydgate. Nabu Press, 2010. Print.

Marie de France, and Mary Lou Martin. *The Fables of Marie de France: An English Translation*. Birmingham, Ala: Summa Publications, 1984. Print.

Phaedrus. *Phædrus His Fables with English Notes*. By William Willymott. Lodon sic: printed for John Osborn, and Tho. Longman, 1728. Print.

Critical Studies

Adrados, Francisco Rodriguez, and Gert-Jan Van Dijk. *History of the Graeco-Latin Fable: Introduction and from the Origins to the Hellenistic Age*. Trans. Leslie A. Ray. Brill Academic Pub, 1999. Print.

Blackham, H. J. *Fable as Literature*. 1st Ed. Athlone Press, 1985. Print.

Holzberg, Niklas. *The Ancient Fable: an Introduction*. Bloomington: Indiana University Press, 2002. Print.

Lerer, Seth. *Children's Literature: a Reader's History, from Aesop to Harry Potter*. Chicago: University of Chicago Press, 2008. Print.

Mann, Jill, and Oxford University Press. *From Aesop to Reynard Beast Literature in Medieval Britain*. Oxford: Oxford University Press, 2009. Print.

Patterson, Annabel M. *Fables of Power: Aesopian Writing and Political History*. Durham: Duke University Press, 1991. Print.

Wheatley, Edward. *Mastering Aesop: Medieval Education, Chaucer, and His Followers*. Gainesville: University Press of Florida, 2000. Print.

Ziolkowski, Jan M. *Talking Animals: Medieval Latin Beast Poetry, 750-1150.* University of Pennsylvania Press, 1993. Print.

How to use this book

The page-by-page vocabularies gloss all but the most common words. We have endeavored to make these glossaries as useful as possible, so there is a lot of repetition. It is our assumption that having too much vocabulary is not as serious a problem as too little, so we have consistently sought to err in that direction. Common words that are not glossed or not glossed in every instance can be found in an appendix in the back, but it is our hope that most readers will not need to use this appendix often. For details on the format of glossing various parts of speech, see "Glossing Conventions" below.

The commentary is almost exclusively grammatical, explaining subordinate clauses, uses of cases, and idioms. A brief grammatical summary details the meaning of the technical terms used in the commentary, although most of these will be familiar to intermediate readers of Latin. A good strategy is to read a passage in Latin, check the glossary for unusual words and consult the commentary as a last resort. We have kept cultural and rhetorical information to a minimum, and it is our expectation that readers will only consult the commentary when something is troubling grammatically. There is considerable repetition in the commentary, and it is meant as a safety net rather than something to be read completely. Our work thus has a more modest aim than a traditional literary commentary.

Glossing Conventions

Adjectives of two and three terminations will be formatted thus:

bonus, -a, -um

facilis, -e.

Single termination adjectives will have the genitive indicated thus:

fallax, **falacis** (*gen.*)

Participles will generally be glossed as a verb, but some present participles (particularly where their verbal force has been weakened) are glossed as nouns or adjectives: e.g.

parens, -entis, *m*: "a parent"

or as a single termination adjective: e.g.,

patiens, -entis (*gen.*): "patient"

Many perfect participles and gerundives are also glossed as adjectives,

erectus, -a, -um: "upright"

periclitabundus, -a, -um: "testing"

Adverbs will be identified as such (*adv.*) only when there is some ambiguity.

Regular infinitives are indicated by conjugation number: e.g.,

laudo (1)

moneo (2)

Where principal parts are predictable, as in the case of most first conjugation verbs, only the conjugation number will be given in the glossary. This format is used even in the case of unpredictable perfect forms, if the word occurring in the text is based on the present stem (present, future, imperfect tenses). Elsewhere the principal parts will be provided in their standard form.

Simple syntactical information such as "+ gen." or "+ inf." will often be cited in the glossary with verbs and adjectives. However, the lexical information given for most words is minimal and sometimes specific to the context.

Grammatical terms used in the commentary

The grammatical terms used in the commentary are organized below according to syntactical category with brief explanations and examples. For more detailed information, see Allen and Greenough, *New Latin Grammar* (available on Perseus) or Charles Bennett *New Latin Grammar* (available on the Latin Library).

1. Uses of Cases

NOMINATIVE

The nominative case is the used for the subject of finite verbs and the predicate of verbs of being, seeming, etc.

GENITIVE

The genitive is commonly used to express a relationship between one noun and another, especially a limiting relationship. Some verbs also take the genitive as their object instead of the accusative.

Material: the genitive denotes what a thing consists of

oviumque satelles canis: "accomplices *consisting of sheep and a dog*"

Objective: the genitive can indicate the object of an action implied by a substantive.

curam gregis: "care *of the flock*"

Partitive: The genitive indicates the whole to which a part belongs.

nil messis: "nothing *of harvest*"

Predicative: A genitive can be used with verbs of being, seeming, etc.

est animi: "he is *of the mind*"

Value: The genitive of is used with verbs of rating and buying.

tanti munera: "gifts *of so much value*"

After verbs and adjectives: The genitive is used to complete the meaning of certain adjectives, such as **reus, -a, -um** ("guilty of"). These will be indicated in the commentary simply as "gen. after *reus.*"

DATIVE

The dative case is chiefly used to indicate the person for whom an action happens or a quality exists.

Indirect Object: the recipient of the action of the verb is put in the dative case.

Jupiter *huic voto* risum dedit: Jupiter gave a smile *to this wish*

Purpose: the dative denotes the object for which something is done.

fora petit *lucro*: seeks the market *for a profit*

Adjectives: certain adjectives such as **aptus, -a, -um** ("suitable to") take the dative. These will be noted in the commentary simply as "dat. after *aptus.*"

Verbs and Compound Verbs: verbs such as **parcere** ("to refrain from") take the dative case, as do many intransitive verbs with a prefix, such as **oppono** ("to place opposite to"). These will be indicated in the commentary simply as "dat. after *parcere.*"

ACCUSATIVE

The accusative case is used for the direct object of transitive verbs, for the subject of an infinitive in indirect statement and other complements of a verb, to indicate place to which, and duration of time.

Predicative: Many verbs can take two accusatives, one the direct object and the other a predicate:

accipitrem ... accipiunt regem: "they accept the hawk as a king"

Subject of Infinitives: In indirect discourse and other expressions that are complemented by an infinitive, the subject of the infinitive is in the accusative case.

aegrum sinit ire: "allows the sick one to go"

Supine: Accusative supines occur after verbs of motion in order to express purpose.

ne libitum faceret: "lest he do what is pleasing"

ABLATIVE

Nouns in the ablative case are used often adverbially, generally expressing motion away from something, instrument, location, and many other relations.

Ablative Absolute: Combined with a participle, adjective, or noun, the ablative conveys the circumstance (time, cause, or condition) of a particular action.

> **inventa jaspide**: "the jasper having been found"

Cause: Cause may be expressed by an ablative with or without a preposition.

> **quaerit...siti**: "sought because of thirst"

Comparison: Comparative adjectives followed by the ablative express comparison.

> **obserat nec minus aure**: "and locks up the home no less *than her ear*"

Manner: Often with *cum*, manner is also denoted by the simple ablative, especially if the noun has an adjective.

> **cursu mendicat inepto**: "she seeks a hiding place *with inept running*"

Means (Instrument): The ablative expresses the means by which an action is accomplished.

> **rigido fodi ore**: "digs *with rigid mouth*"

Place Where: Often denoted by *in* + ablative, but the preposition is commonly omitted in poetry or poetic prose.

> **res utili loco**: "this thing is in a useful place"

Place From Which: The ablative denotes the place a noun has moved from usually with a preposition.

> **ore cadit**: "falls *from his mouth*"

Separation: Separation is expressed with or without a preposition especially with verbs and adjectives of deprivation, freedom, and want.

> **rupisti...rivoque decorum**: "you separated the beauty *from the river*"

Source: The ablative of source is denoted by the ablative with or without a preposition.

> **ore serit**: "sews *from the mouth*"

Specification: The ablative of specification provides details with respect to which anything is or is done.

> **nive canet**: "is white with snow"

Time: Both time when and time within which are denoted by the ablative.

> **die fixo**: "on a fixed day"
>
> **tanto tempore**: "in such a great time"

2. Uses of the Subjunctive

Independent Uses of the Subjunctive

Deliberative questions occur when the speaker wonders what he or she should do.

> **quid agam? quo me conferam?**: "What am I to do? Where am I to take myself?"

Hortatory, Jussive, Prohibition Clauses

Jussive and hortatory subjunctives "urges" some action in a more polite manner than an imperative. "Hortatory" applies to first person ("let us..."); "jussive" applies to second and third person ("may you...," "let her..."); "prohibition" refers to the negative (don't...).

> **virgo ista teneatur**: pres. pass., "let that maiden be held"
>
> **consilium validum requiramus**: "let us seek strong counsel"
>
> **neque respondeas, immo nec prospicias**: "neither answer nor look towards"

The volitive subjunctive expresses a wish for the future:

> **moriar**: "may I die"

Dependent Uses of the Subjunctive

Tenses of the subjunctive in subordinate clauses follow the *sequence of tenses*: present or perfect subjunctive for primary sequence, imperfect or pluperfect for secondary sequence.

tense of main clause	*same time or time after main verb*	*time before main verb*
present or future tense	present subjunctive	perfect subjunctive
past tense	imperfect subjunctive	pluperfect subjunctive

Concessive clauses with *cum* or *licet* take the subjunctive.

> **cum moveant objecta**: "although the accusations move"
>
> **licet instet hiems**: "although winter threatens"

Conditions: The subjunctive is used in future less vivid and contrafactual conditions (see below).

Cum Causal Clauses: When *cum* introduces a causal clause, the subjunctive is used.

cum patrisses: "since you are taking after your father"

Cum Circumstantial Clauses: When *cum* introduces a general circumstance rather than a specific time, the subjunctive is used.

cum pariat fructum: "when it produces fruit"

cum...armet: "since grief equipped"

Proviso clauses with *dum* take the subjunctive.

dum sit..tanta secures: "as long as there is so great an ax"

General temporal clauses take the subjunctive.

dum juvet umbra fugam: "until the shade helps flight" (i.e., whenever that may be)

Indirect commands are an example of a jussive noun clause used as the object of a verb. For more on jussive noun clauses, see below.

supplicuere...ne sine rege forent: "they asked *not to be without a king*"

Indirect questions are formed with the subjunctive following the sequence of tenses and introduced by an interrogative word.

quid reddere possit: "nor has *what she could return*"

quod sequaris iter: "identifies *what road you should flee*"

Indirect statement: The subjunctive is used with *quod* to introduce an alleged statement, as opposed to a statement of fact.

quod sanius esset: "to complain *that it would be healthier*"

Noun Clauses: clauses following certain verbs are introduced with our without ut or ne with the subjunctive, as in indirect commmands.

Reddat ovis panem vult canis: "the dog wishes *that the sheep give back*"

ne fortem societ fragilis vult: "wishes *that the fragile not unite with*"

Purpose Clauses explain the purpose behind the action of the main clause and are usually introduced by *ut* or *ne*.

ut secum murem demergat: "plunges *in order to drown* the mouse"

Relative Clauses of Characteristic: Relative clauses in the subjunctive suggest that the clause does not simply state a fact but rather indicates another type of subjunctive clause such as purpose, result, cause, concession, etc. They are called relative clauses of characteristic for introducing a defining quality or characteristic.

> **quod tibi non faceres**: "what you would not do to yourself"

Result clauses explain the outcome of the action in the main clause, often with an adverb in the main clause signaling the result clause. Result clauses are usually introduced by *ut* or *ut non*.

> **tanti ut …velim**: "so great *so that I wish*"

3. Indirect Statements, Questions, and Commands

Indirect statements are formed with the accusative plus infinitive after verbs of saying, thinking, etc.

> **seque spondet habere**: "and he pledges *that he has*"

Indirect questions are formed with the subjunctive following the sequence of tenses and introduced by an interrogative word:

> **cur detur respice**: "consider *why it is given*"

Indirect Commands are formed with the subjunctive, with or without ut or ne, and are a type of jussive noun clause (see section on the subjunctive above).

> **supplicuere…ne sine rege forent**: "they asked *not to be without a king*"

4. Conditional sentences

Future more vivid conditions express a future *probability*. The protasis (the clause expressing the condition, i.e. the "if" clause) can be the future or future perfect, the apodosis (the clause expressing consequence, i.e. the "then" clause) is the future tense or some equivalent. In English this is expressed with the present tense in the protasis, future tense in the apodosis: "If she comes…then I will go."

> **si venerit Argus, Argum si poteris fallere, victor eris**: "if Argus comes, if you are able to deceive Argus, you will be the victor"

Future less vivid conditions express a future *possibility* and thus use the potential subjunctive in the apodosis and present or perfect subjunctive in the protasis; In English, "If it should…then it would…" or "If it were to…then it would."

> **si nece dignetur murem leo**: "if the lions were to deem the mouse worthy of death"

Contrafactual conditions indicate an untrue premise and conclusion and use the subjunctive mood: imperfect subjunctive for the present (e.g., "if he were now doing this, he would be doing badly"); pluperfect subjunctive for the past (e.g., "if he had done this, he would have done badly").

> **si tibi nunc esset ... viveret nitor**: if he were now here ... the splendor would be living"

5. Rhetorical terms used in the commentary

Alliteration – the repetition of the same consonant.

> **commendat conditque cibos clementia** (Fable 12)

Anaphora – the repetition of the same word or phrase at the beginning of successive clauses.

> **dum...dum...dum** (Fable 1)
>
> **dormit...dormit...dormit** (Fable 16)

Chiasmus – the repetition of words or concepts in reversed order.

> ***Omnia* quae *vici*, me *vincunt omnia*** (Fable 16)

Hendiadys - ("one through two") the use of two nouns instead of a noun and adjective.

> **advena hostis**: "a foreign enemy" (Fable 23)

Litotes - (undestatement) is the use of two negatives to produce a positive.

> **non omni non omnibus omnia**: "not every time should you trust all to not all" (Fable 24)

Personification – the attribution of a personal nature or human characteristic to something nonhuman.

> **sine Marte**: "without war" (Fable 22)

Polysyndeton – excessive use of conjunctions in succession.

> **custosque boum stabulique** (Fable 58)

Transferred epithet - when an epithet is transferred from its proper noun to one with which it is associated.

> **civis in lege novelli**: "citizens new under the law," i.e. "under a new law" (Fable 21)

6. Other terminology

Apocopation – when a word is formed by the removal of the end of a longer word.

> **potuere**: (= **potuerunt**) "they were able"

Figura Etymologica – the same stem used in more than one part of speech.

> **Sic nocet innocuo nocuus, causamque nocendi**: "Thus the harmful harms the harmless, and a cause of harming"

Periphrastic – the use of a participle and a form of the verb *esse* to create a tense.

> **timenda fuit**: (gerundive): "punishment ought to have been feared"; literally, "punishment was that which ought to be feared"

Polyptoton – "many cases" is the use of the same noun in different cases.

> **Sentit enim *fraudes* et *fraudi fraude* resistit**
> **Mente prius texens retia *fraudis*, ait:**
>
> For he senses *trickeries* and resists the *trickery* with a *trick*.
> Weaving the threads *of a trick* in his mind first, he says.

An Important Disclaimer:

This volume is a self-published "Print on Demand" (POD) book, and it has not been vetted or edited in the usual way by publishing professionals. There are sure to be some factual and typographical errors in the text, for which we apologize in advance. The volume is also available only through online distributors, since each book is printed when ordered online. However, this publishing channel and format also account for the low price of the book; and it is a simple matter to make changes when they come to our attention. For this reason, any corrections or suggestions for improvement are welcome and will be addressed as quickly as possible in future versions of the text.

Please e-mail corrections or suggestions to editor@faenumpublishing.com.

About the Authors:

Greta Smith received her PhD in the English Department at Miami University.

Evan Hayes is a graduate in Classics and Philosophy at Miami University and the 2011 Joanna Jackson Goldman Scholar.

Stephen Nimis is an Emeritus Professor of Classics at Miami University and Professor of English and Comparative Literature at the American University in Cairo.

ABBREVIATIONS

abl.	ablative	inf.	infinitive
abs.	absolute	intrans.	intransitive
acc.	accusative	loc.	locative
act.	active	m.	masculine
adj.	adjective	neut.	neuter
adv.	adverb	neg.	negative
apoc.	apocopated	nom.	nominative
appos.	apposition	obj.	object
attend.	attendant	part.	participle
circum.	circumstantial	pass.	passive
com.	command	perf.	perfect
comp.	comparative	pl.	plural
concess.	concessive	plupf.	pluperfect
dat.	dative	pred.	predicate
delib.	deliberative	pres.	present
dep.	deponent	pron.	pronoun
desc.	description	purp.	purpose
dir.	direct	quest.	question
epex.	epexegetic	rel.	relative
f.	feminine	resp.	respect
fut.	future	s.	singular
gen.	genitive	sc.	*scilicet* ("supply")
i.e.	*id est* ("that is")	sep.	separation
imper.	imperative	st.	statement
impf.	imperfect	subj.	subjunctive *or* subject
ind.	indirect	sync.	syncopated

The Elegaic Romulus
Aesop's Fables

Fable 1: De gallo et jaspide

This first fable, the Cock and the Jasp, was moved from the middle of the Phaedrus collection to the beginning of the Romulus, and is lengthened and the moral shifted in order to show how the reader is to approach the rest of the collection. Jill Mann calls this a "fable about fables," and also points out that it was "probably for this reason that it was moved from its relatively late position in the Phaedrus to stand at the very beginning of the Romulus collection" (34). In this fable, while searching through a dungheap for food, a rooster comes upon a precious gem. Rather than keeping the gem, however, the rooster leaves it aside, arguing that it might be valuable to someone else, but as he cannot eat it, it has no value for him. The moral of the fable compares the gem to wisdom, and the reader is told that they are not to behave as the rooster, casting wisdom aside, but to seek out the wisdom in the following fables. The emphasis on wisdom in this fable in the elegiac Romulus certainly allows for a more complex understanding of this fable in relationship to the rest of the fable collection, and the moving of this fable to the beginning of the collection is evidence that the work is aware of itself as a whole, and it encourages the reader as to how they are to read the fables that follow.

Dum rigido fodit ore fimum, dum quaeritat escam,

Dum stupet inventa jaspide, gallus ait:

"Res utili pretiosa loco natique nitoris,

---

esca, -ae *f.*: food, meat
fimus, -i *m.*: dung
fodio (3): to dig, dig out
gallus, -i *m.*: a cock, rooster
invenio (4): to come upon, discover, find
jaspis, -idis *f.*: jasper, gem
locus, -i *m.*: a place, site
natus, -a, -um: inborn, natural

nitor, -is *m.*: brightness, splendor
os, oris *n.*: a mouth
pretiosus, -a -um: of great value, precious
quaerito (1): to seek
res, rei *f.*: a thing
rigidus, -a, -um: stiff, hard
stupeo (2): to be astounded
utilis, -e: useful, helpful

---

dum ... dum ... dum: an example of *anaphora*

rigido ore: abl. of means, "digs *with rigid mouth* i.e. beak"

inventa jaspide: abl. abs., "the jasper having been found"

utili loco: abl. of place where, "in a useful place" i.e. a common place where treasures would not be expected

natique nitoris: gen of description, "a thing *of natural splendor*"

Hac in sorde jacens nil mihi messis habes.

Si tibi nunc esset qui debuit esse repertor,

Quem limus sepelit viveret arte nitor.

Nec tibi convenio, nec tu mihi; nec tibi prosum,

Nec mihi tu prodes, plus amo cara minus."

Tu gallo stolidum, tu jaspide pulcra sophiae

Dona notes: stolido nil sapit ista seges.

---

amo (1): to love, like
ars, artis *f.*: skill, craft, art
carus, -a -um: dear, beloved, precious
convenio (4): to be appropriate to (+ *dat.*)
debeo (2): to owe, be indebted
donum, -i *n.*: a gift, present
habeo (2): to have, hold
jaceo (2): to lie
limus, -i *m.*: filth
messis, messis *m./f.*: harvest, crop
minus: (*adv.*) less
noto (1): to observe, record, understand

plus: (*adv.*) more
prosum, prodesse: be useful to (+ *dat.*)
pulcer, -ra -rum: beautiful
repertor, -oris *m.*: discoverer
sapio (3): to understand, taste
seges, segetis *f.*: crop, harvest
sepelo (3), **sepeli**: to bury
sophia, -ae *f.*: wisdom
sordes, sordis *f.*: filth, dirt
stolidus, -a, -um: dull, stupid
vivo (3): to live, reside

---

messis: gen. partitive after *nil*, "nothing *of harvest*"
si esset: impf. subj. pres. contrafactual protasis, "*if he were* now here,"
repertor: pred. nom., "who ought to be your *discoverer*"
quem: relative pron. antecedent *nitor*, "the splendor *which*"
viveret: impf. subj. contrafactual apodisis, "the splendor *would be living*"
arte: abl. of means, "living *by his art*"
cara minus: "I love *less precious things* more"
tu: i.e. the reader
gallo ... jaspide: abl. of means, "understand *by the rooster ... by the jasper*"
stolidum ... pulcra dona: acc. obj. of *notes*, "you should understand *stupidity* ... you should understand the *beautiful gifts*"
sophiae: gen. of description, "gifts *of wisdom*"
notes: pres. subj. jussive, "you should understand"
stolido: dat. of advantage, "has *for the stupid*"
nil sapit: "has no flavor," note the pun on *sapit*

Fable 2: De lupo et agno

"The Wolf and the Lamb" seems to have been a popular medieval fable; it is occasionally illustrated in manuscripts, and is contained in a number of later translations of the fables. A wolf accuses a lamb of polluting his drinking water, even though the lamb is drinking downstream; the resulting moral is clear: the villainous will find a way to injure the innocent. Interestingly, the end of this moral notes that "these wolves reign in any city," one of only a few fables in the elegiac Romulus to have a political message. These political messages are picked up by fable authors later in the Middle Ages, and particularly in the Renaissance, when, as Annabel Patterson notes, fables are often used for political ends.

Est lupus, est agnus: sitit hic, sitit ille, fluentum

Limite non uno quaerit uterque siti.

In summo bibit amne lupus, bibit agnus in imo.

Hunc timor impugnat verba movente lupo:

"Rupisti potumque mihi rivoque decorem."

Agnus utrumque negat se ratione tuens:

---

agnus, **i** *m.*: a lamb
amnis, **amnis** *m.*: a river
bibo (3): to drink
decor, **-is** *m.*: beauty, decent appearance
fluentum, **-i** *n.*: a stream, river
impugno (1): to attack, assail
imus, **-a**, **-um**: lowest
limes, **limitis** *m.*: a path, track
lupus, **-i** *m.*: a wolf
moveo (2): to move, provoke, disturb
nego (1): to deny, refuse

potus, **-us** *m.*: a drinking
quaero (3): to seek
rivus, **-i** *m.*: a stream
rumpo (3): to break, destroy
sitio (4): to be thirsty
sitis, **sitis** *f.*: thirst
summus, **-a**, **-um**: highest, the top of
timor, **-is** *m.*: fear, dread
unus, **-a** **-um**: alone
uterque, **utraque**, **utrumque**: each (of two)
verbum, **-i** *n.*: a word, proverb

---

limite non uno: abl. of place, "not on the same path"
siti: abl. of cause, "sought *because of thirst*"
in summo ... imo: abl of place where, "*at the highest place* of the river ... *the lowest*"
hunc: i.e. the lamb
movente lupo: abl. abs., "*the wolf moving* these words" i.e. speaking
mihi: dat. of advantage, "you destroyed *for me*"
rivoque: abl. of separation, "the beauty *from the river*"

5

"Nec tibi nec rivo nocui: nam prona supinum

 Nescit iter nec adhuc unda nitore caret."

Sic iterum tonat ore lupus: "Mihi damna minaris?"

 "Non minor," agnus ait. Cui lupus: "Immo facis;

Fecit idem tuus ante pater sex mensibus actis:

 Cum bene patrisses, crimine patris obi."

Agnus ad haec: "Tanto non vixi tempore, praedo."

 Sic tonat: "An loqueris, furcifer?" huncque vorat.

Sic nocet innocuo nocuus, causamque nocendi

---

adhuc: till now
ago, agere, egi, actus (3): to drive, act
bene: well, very
careo (2): to be without (+ *abl.*)
crimen, criminis *n.*: a crime, offense, fault
damnum, -i *n.*: an injury
furcifer, -i *m.*: a rascal
idem, eadem, idem: same, the same
immo: on the contrary, rather
iter, itineris *n.*: a journey, road
iterum: again, a second time
loquor (3): to speak, talk
mensis, mensis *m.*: a month
minor (1): to threaten
nescio (4): to not know
noceo (2): to harm (+ *dat.*)

obeo, obire: to die
os, oris *n.*: a mouth, speech
pater, patris *m.*: a father
patrisso (1): to take after one's father
praedo, praedonis *n.*: a theif
pronus, -a -um: inclined downward
ratio, rationis *f.*: an account, reasoning
sex: six
supinus, -a -um: backwards
tantus, -a, -um: so great, so much
tempus, temporis *n.*: a time
tono (1): to thunder, speak thunderously
tueor (2): to defend
unda, -ae *f.*: a wave
vivo (3), **vixi, victus**: be alive, live
voro (1): to swallow, devour

---

utrumque: "denies *each* (accusation)"
ratione: abl. of means, "defending *with reason*"
prona: nom. agreeing with *unda*, "water *inclined downward*"
supinum iter: obj. of *nescit*, "does not know a *backward journey*"
nitore: abl. of separation after *caret*, "nor does the wave lack *brightness*"
ore: abl. of means, "speaks *with his mouth*"
idem: neut. acc., "did *the same thing*"
sex mensibus actis: abl. abs., "six months having past" i.e. six months ago
cum patrisses: pres. subj. in *cum* causal clause, "since you are taking after your father"
crimine: abl. of cause, "*because of the crime* of your father"
obi: imper., "die!"
tanto tempore: abl. of time where we would expect the accusative, "I have not lived *for so much time*"
an loqueris: "are you still speaking?" expressing indignation

Invenit. Hi regnant qualibet urbe lupi.

causa, **-ae** *f.*: a cause, reason
innocuus, **-a**, **-um**: innocent, harmless
invenio (4): to come upon, discover

nocuus, **-a**, **-um**: hurtful, injurious
regno (1): to reign, rule
urbs, **urbis** *f.*: a city

nocendi: gerund gen. after *causam*, "a reason *for harming*"
qualibet urbe: abl. of place where, "rule *in any city*"

Fable 3: De mure et rana

This fable is particularly grim; a mouse mistakenly trusts a frog to carry her across a lake, but when the frog tries to drown her, the resulting struggle attracts a kite, who devours them both. In this version of the fable, the mouse isn't blamed for her gullibility, rather it is the frog who is chastised in the moral for hindering when he promised to help. Later versions of the fable, such as Robert Henryson's in the 1400s, focus on the mistakes that the mouse made; some versions, such as the earlier Marie de France (1200s), save the mouse from her ominous end to further emphasize the critique of the frog's character.

> Muris iter rumpente lacu, venit obvia muri
>> Rana loquax et opem pacta nocere cupit.
> Omne genus pestis superat mens dissona verbis,
>> Cum sentes animi florida lingua polit.
> Rana sibi murem filo confederat; audet
>> Nectere fune pedem, rumpere fraude fidem.

animus, -i *m.*: mind, intellect	**mens, mentis** *f.*: mind, reason
audeo (2): to dare (+ *inf.*)	**mus, muris** *m./f.*: a mouse
confedero (1): to join X (*acc.*) to Y (*dat.*)	**necto** (3): to tie, bind
cupio (3): to wish, desire (+ *inf.*)	**obvius, -a, -um**: in the way (+ *dat.*)
dissonus, -a, -um: discordant (+ *abl.*)	**omne, omnis**: all, every
fides, fidei *f.*: faith, loyalty	**ops, opis** *f.*: help, resources
filum, fili *n.*: a thread, string	**paciscor**, (3), **pactus sum**: to negotiate
floridus, -a, -um: flowery, florid	**pes, pedis** *m.*: a foot
fraus, fraudis *f.*: fraud, trickery	**pestis, pestis** *f.*: pestilence, destruction
funis, funis *m.*: a rope	**polio** (4): to polish, smooth
genus, generis *n.*: a race, family	**rana, -ae** *f.*: a frog
iter, itineris *n.*: a path	**rumpo** (3): to break
lacus, lacus *m.*: a lake, pond	**sentis, sentis** *m.*: thorns, roughness
lingua, linguae *f.*: a tongue, speech	**supero** (1): to overcome, surpass
loquax, -acis (*gen.*): talkative, loquacious	**venio** (4): to come

rumpente lacu: abl. ab., "*a pond interrupting* the path"
pacta: deponent perf. part. instrumental, "by bargaining"
verbis: abl. of separation after *dissona*, "discordant with its words"
sentes: acc., "smoothes *thorns* of the mind" (i.e. roughness of the mind)
filo: abl. of means, "joins *with a thread*"
fune: abl. of means, "to tie *with a rope*"
fraude: abl. of means, "to destroy *with trickery*"

Pes coit ergo pedi, sed mens a mente recedit.

Ecce natant: trahitur ille, sed illa trahit.

Mergitur ut secum murem demergat; amico

Naufragium faciens naufragat ipsa fides.

Rana studet mergi, sed mus emergit et obstat

Naufragio: vires suggerit ipse timor.

Milvus adest miserumque truci rapit ungue duellum.

Hic jacet, ambo jacent, viscera trita fluunt.

---

adsum: to be present
amicus, amici *m.*: a friend
coeo, coire: fit together with (+ *dat.*)
demergo (3): to sink, plunge
duellum, -i *n.*: a pair
ecce: behold! look!
emergo (3): to rise up out of the water, escape
fluo (3): to flow, proceed from
jaceo (2): to lie, lie down dead
mergo (3): to plunge, drown
milvus, -i *m.*: a bird of prey
miser -a -um: poor, miserable, wretched
nato (1): to swim, float

naufragium, -i *n.*: a shipwreck, ruin
naufrago (1): to be shipwrecked
obsto (1): to oppose, hinder, (+ *dat.*)
rapio (3): to snatch, seize, carry off
recedo (3): to recede, withdraw
studeo (2): to desire (+ *inf.*)
suggero (3): to furnish
traho (3): to draw, drag
tritus, -a, -um: worn
trux, trucis (*gen.*): wild, savage, fierce
unguis, unguis *m.*: a nail, claw, talon
vis, viris *f.*: strength
viscus, visceris *n.*: internal organs

---

mens a mente: abl. of separation, "one mind recedes *from the other mind*" (i.e. their intentions are disparate)

ut demergat: pres. subj. purpose clause, "(the frog) plunges *in order to drown* the mouse"

faciens: pres. part. instrumental, "*by making* a shipwreck"

mergi: pres. pass. inf., "to be submerged"

ungue: abl. of means, "seizes *with its talon*"

hic jacet ... ambo jacent: Note the pun, "this one (the kite) lands ... the two (the mouse and frog) lie dead" i.e. the kite lands and kills them both

Sic pereant qui se prodesse fatentur et obsunt;

Discat in auctorem poenam redire suum.

---

auctor, auctoris *m./f.*: originator
disco (3): to learn
fateor (2): to admit, claim
obsum, obesse: hurt, be a nuisance to

pereo (4): to die, pass away
poena, -ae *f.*: a penalty, punishment
prosum, prodesse: to be useful, benefit
redeo, redire: to return

sic pereant: pres. subj. jussive clause, "may those die!"
se prodesse: pres. inf. in ind. st. after *fatentur*, "claim *that they are helping*"
discat: pres subj. jussive, "let him learn!"
in auctorem: "returns *against its own author*"
poenam redire: pres. inf. in ind. st. after *discat*, "learn *that the punishment returns*"

Fable 4: De cane et ove

Even more so than the Wolf and the Lamb, this fable is explicitly political, and later used to critique legal systems. A lamb is again falsely accused, this time by a dog, who says that she has stolen a loaf of bread. You will note that the court who judges the sheep is made up of rather questionable characters, a kite, a wolf, and a vulture. These animals find the sheep guilty, and she is forced to sell the fleece off her back to repay the debts. Here again the moral does not critique the animal that the reader might think should be questioned-- the dog-- rather it is the false witnesses of the kite, wolf, and vulture who are condemned.

In causam canis urget ovem; sedet arbiter, audit.

Reddat ovis panem vult canis, illa negat.

Pro cane stat milvus, stat vultur, stat lupus: instant

Panem, quem pepigit reddere, reddat ovis.

Reddere non debet, nec habet quid reddere possit;

Et tamen ut reddat arbiter instat ovi.

---

arbiter, arbitri *m.*: a judge
audio (4): to hear, listen
canis, -is *m.*: a dog, hound
causa, causae *f.*: a lawsuit, case, trial
debeo (2): to owe, ought (+ *inf.*)
habeo (2): to have, hold
insto (1): to threaten, demand (+ *dat.*)
lupus, lupi *m.*: a wolf
milvus, -i *m.*: a kite, bird of prey

ovis, ovis *f.*: a sheep
pango (3), **pepigi**: agree upon, pledge (+ *inf.*)
panis, panis *m.*: bread, loaf
reddo (3): to return, give back
sedeo (2): to sit, remain
sto (1): to stand, stand up for
urgeo (2): to press, push
volo, velle: to be willing, wish
vultur, vulturis *m.*: a vulture

in causam: "into court"
reddat: pres. subj. noun clause after vult, "the dog wishes that the sheep *give back.*"
   Note the variations of this verb in the fable.
pro cane: "on behalf of the dog"
reddat: pres. subj. noun clause after *instant*, "they insist *that she return.*"
quid...possit: pres. subj. indirect question, "nor has *what she could* return"
ut reddat: pres. subj. noun clause after *instat*, "insists *that she return it*"
ovi: dat. after instat, "insists *to the sheep* that she return it"

Ergo suum, licet instet hiems, pervendit amictum,

    Et Boream patitur vellere nuda suo.

Saepe fidem falso mendicat inertia teste,

    Saepe dolet pietas criminis arte capi.

amictus, **amictus** *m.*: a cloak, clothing
ars, **artis** *f.*: skill, craft, trick
Boreas, **Boreae** *n.*: the North Wind
capio (3): to take hold, seize
crimen, **criminis** *n.*: a crime, offense
doleo (2): to grieves (+ *inf.*)
ergo: therefore
falsus, **-a**, **-um**: false, deceiving
hiems, **hiemis** *f.*: winter

inertia, **-ae** *f.*: laziness
licet: although
mendico (1): to obtain by importuning
nudus, **-a**, **-um**: nude
patior (3): to suffer, endure
pervendo (3): to sell
pietas, **pietatis** *f.*: responsibility, sense of duty
testis, **testis** *m.*: a witness
vellus, **velleris** *n.*: fleece

instet: pres subj. concessive after *licet*, "although winter *threatens*"
amictum: i.e. her wool
vellere suo: abl. of separation, "nude *from her fleece*"
falso teste: abl. of means, "obtains *with a false witness*"
arte: abl. of means, "by the skill"
capi: pres. pass. inf. complementing *doleo*, "grieves *to be caught*"

Fable 5: De cane carnem ferente

In this familiar fable, a dog carries a piece of meat in his mouth until he sees his reflection in a pool of water. Jealous of the reflection of his own meat, the dog drops the piece in his mouth hoping to be able to grab the larger piece. The moral reminds us not to desire things that are not our own. This fable is perhaps one of the most ancient, referred to by the philosopher Democritus in the 5th century BC. The fable also appears in the 12th century Aberdeen Bestiary, where the dog is illustrated as swimming across a pond with the meat in his mouth. This fable has been reinterpreted with a number of other foods, most often a piece of cheese, which the dog again drops hoping to gain a larger piece; some versions that include the cheese also show the dog seeing the reflection of the moon behind him, which he mistakes as a larger piece of cheese.

Dum canis ore gerit carnem, caro porrigit umbram;

Umbra cohaeret aquis: has canis urget aquas.

Spes canis plus carne cupit, plus faenore signum

Faenoris; os aperit, sic caro spesque perit.

Non igitur debent pro vanis certa relinqui.

Non sua quis avet, mox caret ipse suis.

---

aperio (4): to open	**multum**: much, greatly
aqua, -ae *f.*: water	**os, oris** *n.*: a mouth
aveo, (2): to desire, wish for	**pereo** (4): to be destroyed, go to waste
canis, -is: dog, hound	**plus**: (*adv.*) more
careo (2): to be without	**porrigo** (3): to stretch out, cast
caro, carnis *f.*: meat	**relinquo** (3): to leave behind, abandon
certum, -i *n.*: that which is fixed, certain	**signum, signi** *n.*: an image
cohaereo (2): to clings to (+ *dat.*)	**spes, spei** *f.*: hope, expectation
faenus, fenoris *n.*: profit, gain	**umbra, -ae** *f.*: a shadow
fero, ferre: to carry	**urgeo** (2): to push, press
gero (3): to bear, carry	**vanus, -a, -um**: empty, vain

ore: abl. of means, "carries *in his mouth*"

aquis: dat. after compound verb, "clings *to the water*"

carne... faenore: abl. after *plus*, "more than the meat ... more than the profit"

spes canis... signum faenoris: both subjects of cupit, "the hope of the dog...the image of profit"

relinqui: pres. pass. inf. after *debent*, "certain things ought not *be left behind*"

quis (=quisque): "*whoever* desires"

non sua: "does not desire *his own things*"

suis: abl. of separation after *caret*, "he will be without *his own possessions*"

Fable 6: De ove et capra et juvenca et leone

With possibly one of the largest cast of characters, this fable is the first of many that critique corrupt leaders. The four animals capture a deer, but the lion claims all four shares of the spoils, citing various levels of power in his claim. You will note again that the villainous character isn't blamed in the moral, rather these fables seem to be showing the reader how to navigate a world populated with these villains. The fable suggests that weaker people, here represented by the goat, sheep, and heifer, should not associate with the strong.

> Ut ratione pari fortunae munera sumant,
>
>> Sumunt foedus ovis capra juvenca leo.
>
> Cervus adest, cervum rapiunt. Leo sic ait. "Heres
>
>> Primae partis ero: nam mihi primus honor.
>
> Et mihi defendit partem vis prima secundam,
>
>> Et mihi dat major tertia jura labor.
>
> Et pars quarta meum, nisi sit mea, rumpet amorem."

---

adedo, adesse: to eat up	**munus, muneris** *n.*: duty, gift
amor, amoris *m.*: love	**ovis, ovis** *f.*: a sheep
capra, -ae *f.*: a she-goat	**par, paris** (*gen.*): equal
cervus, -i *m.*: a stag, deer	**pars, partis** *f.*: a part, portion
defendo (3): to defend, guard	**primus, -a, -um**: first, best
foedus, -eris *n.*: a bargain	**publicus, -a, -um**: public, common
fortuna, -ae *f.*: chance, luck, fate	**quattuor**: fourth
heres, heredis *m./f.*: an heir, heiress	**rapio** (3): to destroy, seize
honor, honoris *m.*: honor, respect	**ratio, rationis** *f.*: an account, reckoning
jus, juris *n.*: law, legal system	**rumpo** (3): to break, destroy
juvenca, -ae *f.*: a young cow, heifer	**secundus -a -um**: second, next
labor, laboris *m.*: labor	**sumo** (3): to take up, begin, obtain
leo, leonis *m.*: a lion	**tertius, -a, -um**: third
major, -us: larger, greater	**vis, viris** *f.*: strength

---

ratione pari: abl of manner, "obtain *in equal amount*"
sumant: pres. subj. in purpose clause, "in order to obtain the gifts of fortune"
tertia jura: acc. obj., "gives *the third privileges*"
nisi sit: pres. subj. in fut. less vivid protasis, "unless it be mine"
rumpet: fut. in a "more vivid" apodosis, "will be destroying"

Publica solus habet fortior, ima premens.

Ne fortem societ fragilis vult fabula presens:

Nam fragili fidus nesciet esse potens.

---

fabula, -ae *f.*: story, fable
fidus, -a, -um: faithful, loyal to (+ *dat.*)
fortior, -ius: stronger, more powerful
fortis, -e.: strong
fragilis, -e: brittle, frail
imus, -a, -um: lowest

nescio (4): to not know how to (+ *inf.*)
potens, potentis (*gen.*): powerful, strong
praesens, praesentis (*gen.*): present, at hand
premo (3): to press, press hard
socio (1): to unite, join with (+ *acc.*)
solus, -a, -um: only, single

---

publica: neut. pl. acc., "has *public things*" i.e. common property

ima: neut. pl. acc., "represses *the lowest*"

ne...societ: pres. subj. in noun clause after *vult*, "wishes *that* the fragile *not unite with*"

fabula praesens: i.e. this very fable

fidus: nom. pred., "does not know to be *faithful to*" + dat.

fragili: dat. after *fidus*, "loyal *to the fragile*"

potens: subj. of *nesciet*, "*the powerful* do not know"

Fable 7: De fure uxorem ducente

In this fable, the woman marrying the thief is a frame used to set up the actual fable, which tells how the sun took a bride. This fable about the sun is taken from the Phaedrus collection, where it is called "The Sun who Wished to Wed." The moral remains the same; at first the other planets celebrate when the sun wishes to take a bride, but they soon realize that the bride would double the warmth of the sun, making too much of a good thing. It isn't clear why the author of the elegiac Romulus chooses to frame this fable within the narrative of a woman who married a thief, although this second narrative strengthens the moral by duplicating the situation—again, there would be too much of a not-so-good thing.

> Femina dum nubit furi, vicinia gaudet.
>
> Vir bonus et prudens talia verba movet:
>
> "Sol pepigit sponsam. Jovis aurem terra querelis
>
> Perculit et causam, cur foret aegra, dedit:

---

aeger, -ra, -rum: sick, grieved
auris, auris *f.*: an ear, hearing
bonus, -a, -um: good, honest
causa, -ae *f.*: a cause, reason
do (1) **dedi datus**: to give
duco (3): to lead, command
femina, ae *f.*: a woman, female
fur, furis *m./f.*: a thief, robber
gaudeo (2): to rejoice
Juppiter, Jovis *m.*: Jupiter, Jove
moveo (2): to move, stir
nubo (3): to marry, be married to (+ *dat.*)

pango (3) **pepigi**: to compose, settle upon
percello (3), **-culi**: to strike
prudens, -entis (*gen.*): aware, skilled
querela, -ae *f.*: a complaint, grievance
sol, solis *m.*: sun
sponsa, -ae *f.*: a bride
talis, tale: such, so great
terra, -ae *f.*: earth
uxor, uxoris *f.*: a wife
verbum, -i *n.*: a word, proverb
vicinia, -ae *f.*: neighborhood
vir, -i *m.*: a man, husband

---

uxorem ducente: "leading a wife," i.e. marrying
querelis: abl. of means, "the earth struck *with quarreling*"
cur foret : impf. subj. in ind. quest., "gave reason *why she should be* grieved"

16

'Sole necor solo; quid erit, si creverit alter?

Quid patiar? Quid aget tanta caloris hiems?'"

Hic prohibet sermo laetum praebere favorem,

Qui mala fecerunt vel mala facta parant.

ago (3): to drive, urge	**malum, mali** *n.*:evil
alter, -a, -um: one (of two)	**neco** (1): to kill, murder
calor, caloris *m.*: heat, warmth	**paro** (1): to prepare, furnish
cerno (3), **crevi**: to sift, separate, distinguish	**patior** (3): to suffer
cresco (3), **crevi**: to come forth, be born	**praebeo** (2): to present, show
factum, -i *n.*: a fact, deed	**prohibeo** (2): to hinder, forbid, prevent
favor, favoris *m.*: favor, goodwill	**sermo, sermonis** *m.*: conversation, discussion
hiems, hiemis *f.*: winter, storm	**tantus, -a, -um**: so great, so much
laetus, -a, -um: happy, joyous	

sole solo: abl. of means, "I am slain *by a single sun*"

si creverit: fut. perf. in fut. more vivid protasis, "*if* a second *will have been born*"

caloris hiems: "*a* storm of heat," storms usually occur in winter, hence the (paradoxical) metonymy

praebere: pres. inf. after *prohibet*, "prevents *from showing*"

vel mala: "*even more evil* deeds"

Fable 8: De lupo et grue

The image in this fable is a rather common one; a crane reaches down a wolf's throat to dislodge a stuck bone. This is such a compelling image that it is often illustrated in the fable manuscripts, showing the wolf with its mouth wide open, and just the body of the crane as he works to remove the bone. Once again, this is a lesson in how to live with the wicked; it is the crane who should not have been persuaded by the wolf's empty promises of reward.

> Arta lupum cruciat via gutturis osse retento;
>
> Mendicat medicam, multa daturus, opem.
>
> Grus promissa petit de faucibus osse revulso;
>
> Cui lupus: "an vivis munere tuta meo?

---

artus, -a -um: close, tight
crucio (1): to torment, torture
faux, faucis *f.*: pharynx, throat
grus, gruis *m./f.*: a crane
guttur, -is *n.*: a throat, neck
lupus, -i *m.*: a wolf
medicus, -a, -um: medical
mendico (1): to beg for
multus, -a, -um: much, many

munus, -eris *n.*: a payment, gift
ops, opis *f.*: power, help
os, ossis *n.*: a bone
promitto (3) **-misi, -missum**: to promise
retento (1): to hold fast, restrain
revello (3): to remove, pull away
tutus, -a, -um: safe, prudent
via, -ae *f.*: a way, road
vivo (3): to be alive, live

---

arta ... via: nom., "the narrow passage" i.e. throat
osse retento: abl. abs., "a bone having been stuck"
daturus: fut. act. part., "about to give" i.e. promising to give many things
promissa: neut. pl. acc., "seeks *the things promised*"
osse revulso: abl. abs., "the bone having been removed"
munere meo: abl. of cause, "live safely *from my gift*"

Nonne tuum potui morsu praecidere collum?

Ergo tibi munus sit tua vita meum."

Nil prodest prodesse malis: mens prava malorum

Immemor accepti non timet esse boni.

acceptus, -a -um: welcome, received
bonus, -a, -um: good
collus, -i *m.*: neck, head and neck
immemor, immemoris: forgetful of (+ *gen.*)
malum, -i *n.*: an evil, ill
mens, mentis *f.*: mind
morsus, morsus *m.*: a bite, teeth

nil: nothing
praecido (3): to cut off
pravus, -a, -um: crooked, corrupt
prosum, prodesse: be useful, benefit
timeo (2): to fear (+ *inf.*)
vita, -ae *f.*: life

morsu: abl. of means, "cut off *with my bite*"
sit: pres. subj. jussive, "*let your life be* my payment"
prodesse: pres. inf. subject of *prodest*, "*to benefit* benefits"
malis: dat. after *prodesse*, "to benefit *evil ones*"
malorum: gen. of cause after *prava*, "corrupt *from evils*"
immemor: nom. pred., "fear to be *forgetful of*" + gen.

Fable 9: De duabus canibus

This fable is used by other fable authors, such as Marie de France, to interesting ends because the villain is not clear by the species of animal as it often is in the fables. This also makes it a difficult fable to follow-- one dog welcomes another into her home, but the second dog is quickly tricked into taking care the first dog's young. The sweet-talk of the first dog convinces the other to take the young, and it is these "honeyed words" that are cautioned in the moral.

> De partu querulam, verborum nectare plenam,
>
> Pro cane mota, canis suscipit aede canem.
>
> Haec abit, illa manet; haec cursitat, illa quiescit.
>
> Huic tamen a partu rumpitur illa quies.
>
> Illa redit reddique sibi sub jura precatur;
>
> Obserat haec aurem nec minus aure domum.

---

abeo, abire: depart, go away
canis, canis *m./f.*: a dog, hound
cursito (1): to run
domus, -i *f.*: a house, building
duo -ae: two
jus, juris *n.*: law, legal system
maneo (2): to remain, stay
minus: less
nectar, -aris *n.*: sweetness
obsero (1): to lock, stop up

partus, partus *m.*: a bearing, bringing forth
plenus, -a, -um: full of (+ *abl.*)
precor (1): to beg
querulus, -a, -um: complaining
quies, quietis *f.*: quiet, calm
quiesco (3): to rest, sleep
redeo, redire: return, go back
rumpo (3): to break, destroy
suscipio (3): to undertake
tamen: yet

---

de partu: "complaining *about her bearing*" i.e. her pregancy
querulam ... plenam ... canem: acc., "takes up *a complaining ... full ... dog*"
nectare: abl. after *plenam*, "full of *the sweetness* of words"
mota: perf. part. nom., "she *having been moved* on behalf of the (pregnant) dog
haec ... illa: "the former (the host dog) ... the latter (the guest dog who is pregant)"
    Note the mannered use of these demonstrative terms throughout
huic: dat. of advantage, "that quiet is broken *for this one*" i.e. for the guest dog after
    delivering her young
illa redit ... precatur: "that one (the host dog) returns and begs"
reddi: pres. pass. inf. after *precatur*, "begs (her home) *to be restored*"
haec obserat: "*this one* (the guest dog) *closes* her ear"
aure: abl. comp. after *minus*, "and locks up the home no less *than her ear*"

Plus prece posse minas putat haec, plus bella duobus.

Haec scit posse minas plus prece, bella minis.

Cum dolor hanc armet, plus matrem filius armat;

Cedit sola gregi, causaque justa perit.

Non satis est tutum mellitis credere verbis:

Ex hoc melle solet pestis amara sequi.

---

amarus, -a, -um: bitter, harsh
armo (1): to equip, strengthen
bellum, -i *n.*: war, warfare
causa, -ae *f.*: a cause, reason
cedo (3): to go, pass, concede
credo (3): to trust in (+ *dat.*)
dolor, doloris *m.*: pain, anguish
filius, -i *m.*: a son
grex, gregis *m./f.*: a flock, herd
justus, -a, -um: just
mater, matris *f.*: a mother
mel, mellis *n.*: honey
mellitus, -a, -um: sweetened with honey

mina, -ae *f.*: threats, menaces
pereo (4): to die, pass away
pestis, pestis *f.*: a plague, pestilence
plus: more
prex, precis *f.*: a prayer, request
puto (1): to think, believe
satis: enough, adequately
scio, scire: know, understand
sequor (3): to follow
soleo (2): to be in the habit of (+ *inf.*)
solus, a, um: only, alone
tutus, -a, -um: safe

---

plus ... posse minas: ind. st. after *putat*, "she calculates *that threats are more powerful*"

prece ... duobus: abl. of comp. after *plus*, "threats are more powerful *than prayer ...* that war is more powerful *than those two*" i.e. than threats and prayer"

haec scit: the change of subject is marked only by the contrast in verbs, "now she (the host dog) comes to know that ..." i.e. vs. *putat haec* above

cum ... armet: pres. subj. in cum circumstantial, "*since grief equipped* this one (the host dog)"

gregi: dat. after *cedit*, "alone, she concedes *to the group*" i.e. to the mother and her pup

mellitis verbis: dat. after *credere*, "trust in *sweet words*"

credere: pres. inf. epexegetic after *tutum*, "not sufficiently safe *to believe*" + dat.

sequi: pres. inf. after *solet*, "a plague usually *follows*"

Fable 10: De rustico et colubro

"The Man and the Snake" is essentially the same fable as the preceding two dog fable; a man takes a snake into his home, feeling sorry for the animal because of a particularly harsh winter. The man is rewarded for his hospitality by poison pouring from the snake's mouth. When the man tries to oust the animal, just like the dog, he is attacked. This time, however, it is poison rather than honey that the animal uses to force the man out of his own home.

Dum nive canet humus, glacies dum sopit aquarum

Cursus, in colubrum turbida saevit hiems;

Hunc videt, hunc reficit hominis clementia: ventum

Temperat huic tecto, temperat igne gelu.

Ore serit virus coluber, sic toxicat aedem;

Hospes ait colubro: "non rediturus abi."

---

aedes, -is *f.*: a home
aqua, -ae *f.*: water, sea
cano (3): to be white
clementia, -ae *f.*: mercy, clemency
coluber, colubri *m.*: a snake, serpent
cursus, cursus *m.*: a running
gelu, -us *n.*: frost, ice
glacies, -i *f.*: ice
hiems, hiemis *f.*: winter
homo, hominis *m.*: a man
hospes, hospitis *m.*: a host, guest
humus, -i *f.*: ground, earth
ignis, ignis *m.*: fire
nix, nivis *f.*: snow

os, oris *n.*: a mouth, speech
reficio (3): to rebuild, restore
rusticus, -i *m.*: a peasant, farmer
saevio (4): to rage
sero (3): to sow, plant
sopio (4): to cause to sleep
tectum, tecti *n.*: a roof, house
tempero (1): to temper, make mild
toxico (1): to poison
turbidus, -a, -um: wild, stormy
ventus, -i *m.*: wind
video (2): to see, look at
virus, -i *n.*: venom

---

nive: abl. of specification, "is white *with snow*"
cursus: acc. pl., "puts to sleep *the flowings*"
in colubrum: "rages *against the snake*"
hunc: i.e. the snake
huic: dat., "for this one" i.e. the snake
tecto ... igne: abl. of means, "he makes mild *with his house ... with fire*"
ore: abl. of source, "from the mouth"
non rediturus: fut. act. part., "go away *never to return*"

22

Non exit coluber nec vult exire, sed haeret

    Amplectensque virum sibila dira movet.

Reddere gaudet homo nequam pro melle venenum,

    Pro fructu poenam, pro pietate dolum.

amplector (3): to surround, encircle	**nequam** (*indec. adj.*): vile
dirus, -a, -um: awful, fearful	**pietas, pietatis** *f.*: responsibility
dolus, doli *m.*: a trick, deceit	**poena, -ae** *f.*: a penalty, punishment
exeo, exire: to leave, depart	**reddo** (3): to return, restore
fructus, fructus *m.*: produce, fruit	**sibilum, -i** *n.*: a hissing
gaudeo (2): to be glad, rejoice (+ *inf.*)	**venenum, -i** *n.*: a poison, drug
haereo (2): to stick, adhere	**vir, -i** *m.*: a man, husband
moveo (2): to move	**vult**: be willing, wish (+ *inf.*)

homo nequam: nom. subj., "*a vile man* enjoys"
pro melle: "in return for the honey"

Fable 11: De asino et apro

In this fable it isn't clear what exactly it is that is making the ass laugh, but regardless, the boar is quite unhappy with the mockery. The muddled fable makes it less obvious who the villain is, but the ass is chastised for his mocking.

Audet asellus aprum risu temptare protervo
Audet iners forti dicere: "frater ave."
Vibrat aper pro voce caput: nam verba superbit
Reddere, sed dentem vix tenet ira trucem.

---

aper, apri *m./f.*: a boar, wild boar
asellus, i *m.*: an ass, donkey
asinus, -i *m.*: an ass, donkey
audeo (2): to dare/have (+ *inf.*)
ave: hail!
caput, capitis *n.*: a head, person
dens, dentis *m.*: a tooth, tusk
fortis, forte: strong, powerful, mighty
frater, fratris *m.*: a brother, cousin
iners, inertis (*gen.*): inactive, inert
ira, -ae *f.*: anger

protervus, -a, um: shameless
risus, risus *m.*: laughter
superbio (4): to be too proud to (+ *inf.*)
tempto (1): to test, bribe
teneo (2): to hold
trux, trucis (*gen.*): wild, savage, fierce
verbum, -i *n.*: a word, proverb
vibro (1): to brandish, wave, shake
vix: hardly
vox, vocis *f.*: a voice

---

protervo: abl of means or manner, "tempt *with shameless laughter*"
forti: dat., "speak *to the strong one*"
pro voce: "in place of a voice"

Sus tamen ista movet: "vilem dens nobilis escam
Spernit; desidia tutus es ipse tua."
Non debet stolido laedi prudentia risu,
Nec stolidus doctum debet adire jocis.

adeo, adire: to approach, attack
debeo (2): to ought (+ *inf.*)
desidia, desidiae *f.*: idleness, slackness
doctus, -a, -um: learned, wise
esca, -ae *f.*: food, meat
iste -a -ud: that one (derogatory)
jocus, -i *m.*: a joke, jest
laedo (3): to strike, hurt

nobilis, nobile: haughty
prudentia, -ae *f.*: discretion, wisdom
sperno (3): to scorn, despise, spurn
stolidus, -a -um: dull, stupid
sus, suis *m.*: a hog
tutus, -a, -um: safe
vilis, -e: cheap, common

desidia ... tua: abl. of cause, "safe *because of your idleness*"
stolido risu: abl. of means, "harmed *by stupid laughter*"
laedi: pass. inf. complementing debet, "ought not *to be harmed*"
jocis: abl. of manner, "attack *with jokes*"

25

Fable 12: De mure urbano et rustico

This fable is perhaps the most commonly known of the entire collection, even today. It is used and elaborated upon throughout the Middle Ages, playing a prominent part in both Marie de France's and Henryson's collections. Although considerably lengthened in these other collections, even here the fable is one of the longest in the elegiac Romulus. It seems to have been a particular favorite of the medieval reader, as a number of manuscript copies show marginal markings beside lines which they must have found significant. These marked lines reveal various moral lessons within the body of the fable (see lines 3-4, 9-10, and 20-24).

Rusticus urbanum mus murem suscipit, edem

   Commodat et mensam, mensaque mente minor:

In mensa tenui satis est immensa voluntas,

   Nobilitat viles frons generosa dapes.

Facto fine cibis urbanum rusticus audit;

   Urbani socius tendit in urbis opes.

---

audio (4): to hear, listen	**mus, muris** *m./f.*: a mouse
cibus, cibi *m.*: food, fare	**nobilito** (1): to ennoble
commodo (1): to provide	**ops, opis** *f.*: resources, wealth
dapis, -is *f.* feast, banquet	**rusticus, -a, -um**: country
edes, edis *f.*: food	**socius, -i** *m.*: a companion, ally
finis, finis *m./f.*: an end	**suscipio** (3): to receive
frons, frontis *m./f.*: look, front	**tendo** (3): to go
generosus, -a, -um: noble	**tenuis, tenue**: thin, fine
immensus, -a, -um: immeasurable, immense	**urbanus, -a, -um**: of the city
mens, mentis *f.*: mind, intention	**urbs, urbis** *f.*: a city
mensa, mensae *f.*: a meal	**vilis, -e**: cheap, common
metior (4): to measure	**voluntas, voluntatis** *f.*: will, good will
minus, -or: less	

---

mus murem: note the use of *polyptoton* in the opening lines and elsewhere

mente: abl. of comparison, "less *than his intention*"

in mensa tenui ... immensa voluptas: "at a thin table (poor table) ... an immense good will" note the pun on *in mensa* and *immensa*

frons gernerosa: nom., "his noble intention"

facto fine: abl. absolute, "*the end* of the food *having been made*"

urbani socius: "the friend of the city mouse" i.e. the country mouse

in urbis opes: "to the riches of the city"

26

Ecce penum subeunt, inseruit amicus amico,

   Invigilat mensae, fercula mensa gerit.

commendat conditque cibos clementia vultus,

   Convivam satiat plus dape frontis honor.

Ecce sere clavis immurmurat, hostia latrant;

   Ambo timent, fugiunt ambo, nec ambo latent.

Hic latet, hic latebras cursu mendicat inepto,

   Assuitur muro reptile muris onus.

Blanda, penu clauso, parcit fortuna timori;

   Ille tamen febrit, teste tremore timet.

---

amicus, amici *m.*: a friend
assuo (3): to sew on, cling to
blandus, -a -um: flattering, gentle
claudo (3): to close, shut
clavis, -is *f.*: door-key
clementia, -ae *f.*: gentleness, mildness, calm
commendo (1): to entrust
condio (4): to spice, season, resender pleasant
conviva, -ae *m./f.*: a guest, table companion
cursus, cursus *m.*: a running
dapis, -is *f.*: a feast, banquet
ecce: behold!
febrio (4): to become ill, catch a fever
ferculum, -i *n.*: food
fortuna, fortunae *f.*: chance, luck
frons, frontis *m./f.*: a forehead, face
fugio (3): to flee
gero (3): to bear, carry
honor, honoris *m.*: honor
hostia, -orum *n.*: enemy
immurmuro (1): to murmur

ineptus, -a, -um: silly, foolish
inservio (4): to take care of, serve (+ *dat.*)
invigilo (1): to watch (over) diligently (+ *dat.*)
latebra, -ae *f.*: a hiding place
lateo (2) **latui**: lie hidden
latro (1): to bark, bark at
mendico (1): to beg for, seek
murus, -i *m.*: a wall
onus, oneris *n.*: load, weight
parco (3): to spare (+ *dat.*)
penus, -us *n.*: a pantry, storeroom
reptilis, -e: creeping
satio (1): to satisfy
serus, -a -um: late, too late
subeo (4): enter (+ *acc.*)
testis, testis *m.*: witness
timeo (2): to fear
timor, timoris *m.*: fear, dread
tremor, tremoris *m.*: trembling, shuddering
vultus, vultus *m.*: a face, expression, looks

---

commendat ... clementia: note the alliteration
clementia vultus: "*the gentleness of his face* commends"
dape: abl. of comp. after *plus*, "satisfies more than *the food*"
cursu inepto: abl. of manner, "seeks *with foolish running*"
muro: dat. after compound verb, "clings *to the wall*"
muris: gen., "burden *of the mouse*" i.e. his body
penu clauso: abl. abs., "storeroom having been closed"
teste tremore: abl. abs., "with trembling as a witness"

Exit qui latuit, timidum sic lenit amicum:

"Gaude, carpe cibos, haec sapit esca favum."

Fatur qui timuit: "latet hoc in melle venenum,

Fellitumque metu non puto dulce bonum;

Quam timor obnubit, non est sincera voluptas;

Non est sollicito dulcis in ore favus.

Rodere malo fabam quam cura perpete rodi,

Degenerare cibos cura diurna facit.

His opibus gaude, qui gaudes turbine mentis,

Pauperiem ditet pax opulenta mihi.

---

bonum, boni *n.*: good, good thing
carpo (3): to seize, gather
cura, -ae *f.*: concern, worry
degenero (1): to deteriorate, decline
dito (1): to enrich
diurnus, -a, -um: by day, daily
dulce, -e *n.*: sweet
exeo, exire: to come out
faba, -ae *f.*: bean
favus, -i *m.*: honeycomb
fellitus, -a, -um: embittered
for (1): to speak, talk, say
lenio (4): to calm
malo, malle: prefer to (+ *inf.*)
mel, mellis *n.*: honey
metus, metus *m.*: fear

obnubo (3): to veil, cover
opulentus, a -um: wealthy, rich in wealth
os, oris *n.*: mouth
pauperies, pauperiei *f.*: poverty
pax, pacis *f.*: peace
perpes, perpetis (*gen.*): continuous, lasting
puto (1): to think, believe
rodo (3): to gnaw
sapio (3): to taste of (+ *acc.*)
sincerus, -a -um: clean, pure
sollicitus, -a, -um: worried, troubled
timidus, -a, -um: timid, cowardly
turben, -inis *n.*: whirlwind
venenum, -i *n.*: poison
voluptas, voluptatis *f.*: pleasure

---

metu: abl., "embittered *by fear*"

dulce: acc. pred., "a good thing to be *sweet*"

sollicito ... in ore: abl., "in a troubled mouth"

dulcis: nom. pred., "is not *sweet*"

cura perpete: abl., "gnawed *by perpetual care*"

rodere ... rodi: pres. inf. pass. complementing *malo*, "prefer *to gnaw* than *to be gnawed*"

degenerare: pres. inf. after causative *facit*, "causes food *to deteriorate*"

hic opibus: abl. after *gaude*, "enjoy *these riches*"

turbine: abl. after *gaudes*, "you who rejoice in *this whirlwind*"

ditet: pres subj. jussive, "let peace enrich"

Haec bona solus habe, quae sunt tibi dulcia soli,

    Det pretium dapibus vita quieta meis."

Finit verba, redit. Praeponit tuta timendis,

    Et quia summa timet, tutius ima petit.

Pauperies, si laeta venit, tutissima res est.

    Tristior immensas pauperat usus opes.

bonum, **-i** *n.*: good, good thing
dapis, **-is** *f.*: meal
finio (4): to finish
habeo (2): to have
immensus, **-a**, **-um**: immeasurable
imus, **-a**, **-um**: lowest, deepest
laetus, **-a**, **um**: happy, joyful
paupero (1): to make poor, diminish in value
peto (3): to reach towards, make for
praepono (3): to place X (*acc.*) before Y (*abl.*)

pretium, **-i** *n.*: price, value, worth
quietus, **-a**, **-um**: quiet, tranquil, calm
redeo, **redire**: return, go back
solus, **a**, **-um**: only
summus, **-a**, **-um**: highest
tristis, **triste**: sad
tutus, **-a** **-um**: safe
usus, **usus** *m.*: use, enjoyment, experience
venio (4): to come
vita, **-ae** *f.*: life

soli: dat., "to you *alone*"
det: pres. subj. jussive, "may quiet *give* value"
timendis: abl. gerundive, "before *things that must be feared*"

29

Fable 13: De vulpe et aquila

Our modern conceptions of the eagle as a noble animal make this fable confusing; here it is the eagle who is the villain and the fox who is the virtuous character. The eagle has stolen the fox's young, but the fox, ever wily, builds a fire at the base of the tree in order to smoke out the eagle, and retrieve her kits (although it would seem that she also puts them in danger in the process). This moral is a bit more of a general lesson, as it points out the danger in the greater hurting the lesser, as even weaker are capable of inflicting harm.

Dum vulpes aquilam pro rapta prole perungit

Melle precum, praedam reddere nescit avis.

Praeda gemit nidique timet cibus esse gulosi,

Sed redimit natos utilis arte parens.

Arboreum zonat stipulis et vimine truncum,

In stipulam docto dirigit ore facem.

---

aquila, -ae *m./f.*: an eagle
arboreus, -a, -um: of a tree
ars, artis *f.*: skill, trick
avis, avis *f.*: a bird
dirigo (3): to arrange, direct
doctus, -a, -um: learned, skilled
fax, facis *f.*: a torch, fire
gemo (3): to moan, groan, lament
gulosus, -a, -um: gluttonous
mel, mellis *n.*: honey
natus, -i *m.*: a son, child
nescio (4): to not know (+ *inf.*)
nidus, nidi *m.*: a nest
os, oris *n.*: a mouth

parens, parentis *m./f.*: parent, father, mother
perungo (3): to anoint, smear
praeda, -ae *f.*: booty, loot, spoils
prex, precis *f.*: a prayer
proles, prolis *f.*: offspring
rapio (3) **rapui, raptus**: snatch, seize
reddo (3): to return, restore
redimo (3): to recover
stipula,-ae *f.*: a stalk, reed played on as a pipe
truncus, -i *m.*: a trunk (of a tree)
utilis, utile: useful, practical
vimen, viminis *n.*: a twig, shoot
vulpes, vulpis *f.*: a fox
zono (1): to bind, encircle

---

pro rapta prole: "for the sake of her stolen offspring"
melle: abl., "smears *with the honey* of prayers"
cibus: nom. pred., "fears to become *food*"
arte: abl. of means, "redeems *with skill*"
stipulis ... vimine: abl. of means, "encircles *with stalks ... with twig*"
docto ore: abl. of means, "directs *with her skilled mouth*"

In pullos aquilae conjurat copia fumi;

    Hunc tamen et vulpem provida placat avis.

Non sit qui studeat, quia major, obesse minori,

    Cum bene majori possit obesse minor.

conjuro (1): to conspire	**obsum, obesse**: hurt (+ *dat.*)
copia, -ae *f.*: plenty, abundance	**placo** (1): to appease, placate, reconcile
fumus, -i *m.*: smoke, steam	**providus, -a, -um**: forward-looking
major, -us: larger, greater	**pullus, pulli** *m.*: a young hen
minor, -us: smaller, littler	**studeo** (2): to desire, be eager to (+ *inf.*)

non sit: pres. subj. jussive clause, "let there be no one!"

qui studeat: pres. subj. relative clause of characteristic, "no one *who he is eager*"

cum possit: pres. subj. causal, "since he is able to hurt"

Fable 14: De aquila et testudine

There is a third character in this fable, the raven, who does most of the speaking. The eagle has picked up a tortoise, but seems to be unsure if any food is to be found in the hard shell. It is the raven that advises the eagle to drop the tortoise to uncover its fleshy innards. The moral of this fable is opaque, with its warning against being overwhelmed by "the tongue's whirlwind." The only explanation here is that the raven is giving this advice so that he can grab the flesh of the tortoise away from eagle, and the moral is warning the eagle from taking the advice. Interestingly, in later versions of the fable the tortoise has been replaced by a mollusk or other shelled animal, often depicted as a snail. It seems that, when the elegiac Romulus was put into print by Heinrich Steinhowel in the 1400s, the translator and illustrator misunderstood what the shelled animal that the eagle carried was, and the mollusk or snail was the only animal they could think of with a hard outer shell. It is this mistaken illustration that is included here.

Pes aquilae, praedo testudinis, aëra findit.

Hanc sua conca tegit, cornua longa patent.

Hoc monitu cornix aquilam praemunit: "Ineptum

Fers onus, at fiet utile, crede mihi;

Quod geris in conca, cibus est: tibi surripit illum

---

aquila, -ae *m./f.*: an eagle
aër, aëris *n.*: air, sky, cloud
conca, -ae *f.*: a shell
cornix, cornicis *f.*: a crow
cornu, cornus *n.*: a horn, talon
credo (3): to trust (+ *dat.*)
fero, ferre: to bring, bear
findo (3): to split, divide
fio, fieri: to be made, become
gero (3): to bear, carry
ineptus, -a, -um: silly, foolish

longus, -a, -um: long
monitus, monitus *m.*: a warning
onus, oneris *n.*: load, cargo
pateo (2): to lie exposed
pes, pedis *m.*: a foot
praedo, -onis *n.*: a plunderer
praemunio (4): to fortify, warn
surripio (3): to take away from, steal (+ *dat.*)
tego (3): to cover, protect
testudo, testudinis *f.*: a tortoise
utilis, utile: useful

aëra: acc. pl., "split *the airs*"
hanc: "cover *her*" i.e. the tortoise
cornua longa: "*the long talons* (of the eagle) are exposed" i.e. ready to attack
fers: 2 sing. of ferro, "you are carrying"
fiet: fut., "*it will become* useful"

Conca cibum; concam frange cibusque cadet.

Ut concam lanies, pro viribus utere sensu;

Hanc, si celsa cadat, saxea franget humus."

Decipientis homo subversus turbine linguae

Corruit; et fortes ista procella rapit.

cado (3): to fall	**procella, -ae** *f.*: a storm
celsus, -a, -um: high	**rapio** (3): to snatch, seize
corruo (3): to tumble down, sink	**saxeus, -a, -um**: rocky, stony
decipio (3): to cheat, deceive	**sensus, sensus** *m.*: feeling, sense
fortis, forte: strong, bold	**subverto** (3) **-verti, -versus**: overturn
frango (3): to break, shatter	**turben, -inis** *n.*: a whirlwind
homo, hominis *m.*: a man	**utor, uti, usus sum** (3): to use (+ *abl.*)
humus, -i *f.*: ground	**vis, viris** *f.*: strength
lanio (1): to tear	

cadet: fut., "the food *will fall*"

ut…lanies: pres. subj. in purpose clause, "use your sense *in order to tear*"

pro viribus: "instead of strength"

utere: pres. imper., "use!" + abl.

si cadat: pres. subj. in future less vivid protasis, "if it were to fall"

celsa: nom., "if she falls *while on high*""

franget: pres. subj. in future less vivid apodosis, "the ground *would break*"

turbine linguae: "by the whirlwind of the tongue" i.e. by deceptive rhetoric

decipientis: pres. part. gen., "the tongue *of the deceiving one*"

Fable 15: De vulpe et corvo

The story line of this fable may seem quite familiar-- a fox appeals to a crow's pride by complimenting his song, and in doing so convinces him to sing again so the fox can snatch the cheese that is in his beak. This basic conceit is picked up, and significantly elaborated upon, by Chaucer in his Nun's Priest's Tale, where the fox takes advantage of the rooster's pride to convince him to sing with his eyes closed, so that the fox can grab the bird. It is often argued that Chaucer takes his fable from the Reynardian beast epics, but reading this fable will make it clear that it should also be considered as one of Chaucer's influences.

Vulpe gerente famem, corvum gerit arbor et escam

Ore gerens corvus, vulpe loquente, silet.

"Corve, decore decens, cignum candore peraequas;

Si cantu placeas, plus ave quaque places."

---

arbor, -is *f.*: a tree
candor, -is *m.*: whiteness
cantus, cantus *m.*: a song, chant, singing
cignus, -i *m.*: a swan
corvus, -i *m.*: a crow
decens: pleasing
decor, -is *m.*: beauty, good looks
esca, -ae *f.*: food, meat
fames, famis *f.*: hunger

gero (3): to carry, bear
loquor (3): to speak, tell
os, oris *n.*: a mouth
peraequo (1): to equal
placeo (2): to please, satisfy
placo (1): to soothe
sileo (2): to be silent
vulpes, vulpis *f.*: a fox

---

vulpe gerente: abl. abs., "*a fox bearing* hunger" being hungry. Note the three different meanings of *gero* in these two lines, an example of *antanaklasis*

ore: abl. of place where, "carrying *in his mouth*"

vulpe loquente: abl. abs., "the fox speaking"

candore: abl. of specification, "you equal *in whiteness*"

si placeas ... places: both verbs are pres. subj. in a future less vivid condition, "if you would please me ... you would soothe me" but from different verbs (*placeo* and *placo*), an example of *figura etymologica*. Note the mannered use of multiple forms of *placeo* in these three lines

Credit avis pictaeque placent preludia linguae;

Dum canit ut placeat, caseus ore cadit.

Hoc fruitur vulpes, insurgunt taedia corvo;

Asperat in medio damna dolore pudor.

Fellitum patitur risum quem mellit inanis

Gloria; vera parit taedia falsus honor.

aspero (1): to sharpen, exacerbate	**insurgo** (3): to rise up
cano (3): to sing	**lingua**, -ae *f.*: tongue, speech
caseus, -i *m.*: cheese	**medium, medi(i)** *n.*: middle
damnum, -i *n.*: a lost possession	**mello** (3): to delight
dolor, doloris *m.*: pain	**pario** (3): bear, beget
falsus, -a, -**um**: wrong, deceptive	**patior** (3): to suffer
fellitus, -a, -**um**: embittered	**pictus**, -a, -**um**: painted, deceptive
fruror (3): to enjoy (+ *abl.*)	**preludium**, -ii *n.*: prelude, preliminary
gloria, -ae *f.*: glory, fame	**pudor, pudoris** *m.*: decency, shame
honor, -is *m.*: honor	**risus**, -us *m.*: laughter
inanis, inane: void, empty, foolish	**taedium**, -i *n.*: weariness, aversion

placent: pres. of *placeo*, not subjunctive, "the preludes *are pleasing*"

preludia: nom. subject of *placent*, referring to the words of the fox, although a "prelude" is usually musical

ut placeat: pres subj. purpose clause, "in order to give pleasure"

ore: abl of place from which, "falls *from his mouth*"

Fable 16: De leone et apro et tauro et asello

Again, the cast of characters in this fable is much greater than just the lion and the boar. In fact, it seems like all of the animals from the earlier "The Lion, the She-Goat, the Sheep, and the Heifer" have come back to punish the lion for his wrongdoing. The lion has now aged, and all of these animals are going to punish him for his tyranny, the cow goring him with his horns, a boar also spearing him, and an ass dealing a swift kick. The moral is just as expected; the lion should have behaved in his younger age.

Irretit miserum gravitas annosa leonem,

Inglaciat corpus corque senile gelu.

Instat aper, pensat veteri pro vulnere vulnus;

Frontis eum telo taurus utroque fodit;

Saevit asellus iners et frontem calce sigillat.

Haec solo gemitu vindicat acta leo:

---

actum, **-i** *n.*: an act, deed
annosus, -a, -**um**: aged, old
aper, **apri** *m./f.*: a boar
asellus, **-i** *m.*: a donkey
calx, **calcis** *m./f.*: a heel
cor, **cordis** *n.*: a heart
corpus, **corporis** *n.*: a body, person
fodio (3): to dig, stab
frons, **frontis** *m./f.*: a forehead
gelu, **-us** *n.*: frost, ice
gemitus, **gemitus** *m.*: a groan
gravitas, **gravitatis** *f.*: a weight, gravity
iners, **inertis** (*gen.*): helpless, weak
inglacio (1): to freeze
insto (1): to threaten, approach

irretio (4): to entangle, hinder
leo, **leonis** *m.*: a lion
miser, -a -**um**: poor, miserable, wretched
penso (1): to pay/punish for
saevo (4): to rage
senilis, **senile**: aged
sigillo (1): to seal, mark
solus, -a, -**um**: only, single, alone
taurus, **-i** *m.*: a bull
telum, **-i** *n.*: a weapon, dart, spear
uterque, **-aque**, **-umque**: each of two
veter, -a, -**um**: old
vindico (1): to vindicate, avenge
vulnus, **vulneris** *n.*: a wound

---

senile gelu: "an old coldness" i.e. the cold of old age, a transferred epithet
veteri pro vulnere: "in return for an old wound"
eum: i.e. the lion
utroque telo: abl. of means, "stabs *with both of the horns* of his forehead"
calce: abl. of means, "marks *with his heel*"
solo gemitu: abl. of means, "avenges *with only a groan*" i.e. with no deeds

"Omnia quae vici, me vincunt omnia. Dormit

Vis mea, dormit honor, dormit honoris opus.

Cui nocui, nocet ille mihi, multisque peperci,

Quae mihi non parcunt, pro pietate nocent."

Hunc timeat casum qui se non fulcit amico,

Nec dare vult felix, quam miser optat, opem.

---

amicus, -i *m.*: a friend
casus, casus *m.*: a fall, chance/fortune
dormio (4): to sleep
felix, felicis (*gen.*): happy, lucky
fulcio (4): to prop up, support
multus, -a, -um: many
noceo (2): to harm, hurt, injure (+ *dat.*)
ops, opis *f.*: power, help

opto (1): to choose, wish
opus, operis *n.*: work
parco (3) **peperci, parsus**: to spare (+ *dat.*)
pietas, pietatis *f.*: mercy
timeo (2): to fear, dread, be afraid
vinco (3), **vici, victus**: conquer, defeat
vult: be willing, wish (+ *inf.*)

---

omnium ... omnia: note *chiasmus* word order with reversal of voice from active to passive. See also below *cui ... mihi*
dormit ... dormit: an example of *anaphora*
pro pietate: "in return for mercy"
timeat: pres. subj. jussive, "let him fear" + dat.
amico: abl. of means, "support *with a friend*"
quam: antecedent *opem*, "the aid *which* he seeks"

Fable 17: De asino et catulo et domino

Providing one of the most comical images of the fables, here an ass is jealous of the attention that the puppy receives, and jumps on his master just as the puppy does, hoping to receive some of this attention himself. Of course, this is not the place of the ass, and the moral confirms that it is not wise to try to live outside of the station that nature has dealt them.

Murmuris et caudae studio testatur amorem,

Nunc lingua catulus, nunc pede palpat erum.

Gaudet erus comitque canem comitemque ciborum

Efficit; alludit turba ministra cani.

Arte pari similesque cibos similemque favorem

Lucrari cupiens inquit asellus iners:

"Me catulo praefert vitae nitor, utile tergum,

---

alludo (3): to frolic, play
amor, -is *m.*: love, affection
ars, artis *f.*: skill, manner
asinus, -i *m.*: an ass, donkey
canis, -is *m.*: a dog, hound
catulus, -i *m.*: a young dog, puppy
cauda, caudae *f.*: a tail
cibus, -i *m.*: food
comes, comitis *m./f.*: a sharer, companion
como (3): to make beautiful, embellish
cupio (3): to wish, desire, want
dominus, -i *m.*: an owner, master
efficio (3): to make X (*acc.*) Y (*acc.*)
erus, -i *m.*: a master, owner
favor, favoris *m.*: favor
gaudeo (2): to be glad, rejoice

lucror (1): to gain, win
minister, -tra, -trum: ministering
murmur, -is *n.*: a mutter, whisper, growl
nitor, -is *m.*: brightness, splendor
palpo (1): to stroke
par, paris (*gen.*): equal (to), a match for
pes, pedis *m.*: a foot
praefero, praeferre, praetuli, praelatus: place X (*acc.*) before Y (*dat.*)
similis, simile: like, similar
studium, -i *n.*: eagerness, enthusiasm
tergum, -i *n.*: back, rear
testor (1): to give as evidence
turba, -ae *f.*: a crowd
utilis, utile: useful
vita, -ae. *f.*: life

---

studio: abl. of manner, "testifies *with the eagerness of*" + gen.
lingua ... pede: abl. of manner, "strikes *with his tongue ... with his foot*"
comitem: acc. pred., "makes him *a sharer*"
cani: abl. of association, "plays *with the dog*"
arte pari: abl., "in a similar manner" note the *variatio* of *pari ... similes*
lucrari: pres. inf. dep. after *cupiens*, "wishing *to win*"
catulo: dat. after *praefert*: " place me before *the puppy*"
nitor ... tergum: nom. subjects of *praefert*

Nec placeo fructu, sed placet ille joco.

Ludam: lude places." Sic ludit tempore viso,

Ut ludo placeat, ludit et instat ero.

Blandiri putat ore tonans, umerisque priorum

Pressis mole pedum se putat esse pium.

Clamat erus, vult clamor opem; subit ordo clientum.

Multa domat multo verbere clava reum.

Quod natura negat, nemo feliciter audet:

Displicet inprudens unde placere putat.

---

audeo (2): to intend, dare
blandior (4): to flatter
clamo (1): to proclaim, declare, cry
clamor, -is *m.*: a shout
clava, -ae *f.*: a club, staff
cliens, clientis *m./f.*: a client, dependent
displiceo (2): to displease
domo (1): to subdue, master
feliciter: happily
fructus, fructus *m.*: crops, fruit, reward
inprudens, -entis (*gen.*): ignorant
jocus, -i *m.*: a joke
ludo (3): to play, mock
ludus, -i *m.*: a game, play
moles, molis *f.*: a large mass
multus, -a -um: much, many
natura, -ae *f.*: nature

nego (1): to deny
ops, opis *f.*: power, might
ordo, ordinis *m.*: a row, order
os, oris *n.*: a mouth
pius, -a, -um: faithful, devoted, pious
placeo (2): to please
pressus, -a, -um: firmly planted, deliberate
prior, prius: ahead, in front
puto (1): to think
reus, -i *m.*: guilty one, culprit
subeo (4): go to support
tempus, temporis *n.*: time
tono (1): to thunder
umerus, -i *m.*: upper arm, shoulder
verber, verberis *n.*: lash, a beating
video (2), **vidi, visus**: see

---

fructu ... joco: abl. of means, "pleases *with fruit ... with a joke*"
ludam: fut., " I will play," note the mannered variations on *ludo* and *ludus*
lude: voc., "you are pleasing, *O play*"
tempore viso: abl. abs., "an occasion having been seen"
ut...placeat: pres. subj. purpose clause, "in order to please"
ero: dat. after *instant*, "he approaches *the master*"
blandiri: pres. inf. dep. after putat, "he supposes *to flatter*"
tonans: pres. part. instrumental, "*by thundering* with his mouth"
umeris pressis: abl. abs., "with the shoulders pressed down"
priorum ... pedum: gen. pl., "with the mass *of his forefeet*"
pium: acc. pred., "thinks himself to be *faithful*"
multa ... clava: nom. s. subject, "many a club"
multo verbere: abl. of means, "with much beating"

Fable 18: De leone et mure

Aside from the two mice fables, the fable of the lion and the mouse must be one of the most retold (again, even today) of the collection. The lion spares the mouse, and in turn, the mouse nibbles a net that has ensnared the lion. This moral states that even the smallest of creatures can be useful to the greatest, but other medieval versions of the fable play with this moral. Robert Henryson uses this fable as the central in his collection, and although the lion does spare the mouse, in this version of the fable he goes on to rampage the countryside, devouring dozens. Here, the moral shows that the greatest may not be worth helping.

> Frigida sopito blanditur silva leoni,
>
>   Cursitat hic murum, ludere prompta, cohors.
>
> Pressus mure, leo murem rapit; ille precatur,
>
>   Ille precem librat, supplicat ira preci.
>
> Haec tamen ante movet animo: "Quid, mure perempto,
>
>   Laudis emes? Summos vincere parva pudet.

animus, animi *m.*: mind	**parvus, -a -um**: small, little
blandior (3): to soothe	**perimo** (3) **-emi, -emptus**: to kill, destroy
cohors, cohortis *f.*: a court, attendants	**precor** (1): to beg, pray
cursito (1): to run	**premo** (3) **presi, pressus**: press, press hard
emo (3): to buy, gain	**prex, precis** *f.*: a prayer, request
frigidus, -a -um: cold, cool	**promptus, -a -um**: eager (+ *inf.*)
ira, -ae *f.*: anger, wrath	**pudet** (2): to shame, make ashamed
laus, laudis *f.*: praise	**rapio** (3): to snatch, seize
leo, -onis *m.*: a lion	**silva, -ae** *f.*: wood, forest
libro (1): to balance, weigh	**sopitus, -a, -um**: sleeping
moveo (2): to move, stir	**summus, -a, -um**: highest, greatest
murus, muri *m.*: a wall, city wall	**supplico** (1): to yield to (+ *dat.*)
mus, muris *m./f.*: a mouse	

frigida ... silva: nom. subject, "a cold forest"

sopito... leoni: dat. after *blanditur*, "soothes *the sleeping lion*"

mure: abl. of means, "having been pressed *by the mouse*" Note the *polyptoton* here and play of *mus* and *murus*

quid ... laudis: "*what of praise* will you win?"

haec: neut. pl. acc., "he moves *these things* in his mind" i.e. he ponders these things

mure perempto: abl. abs., "a mouse having been killed"

vincere: pres. inf. subject of *pudet*, "*to conquer* small ones is shameful"

40

Si nece dignetur murem leo, nonne leoni

    Dedecus et muri coeperit esse decus?

Si vincat minimum summus, sic vincere vinci est.

    Vincere posse decet, vincere crimen habet.

Sit tamen esse decus, sit laus sic vincere: laus haec

    Et decus hoc minimo fiet ab hoste minus.

De pretio victi pendet victoria: victor

    Tantus erit, victi gloria quanta fuit."

Mus abit et grates reddit, si reddere possit

    Spondet opem. Solus fit mora parva dies.

---

abeo, abire: to depart
coepio (3), **coepi, coeptus**: to begin
crimen, criminis *n.*: sin, crime
decet (2): it is fitting
decus, decoris *n.*: glory, honor
dedecus, dedecoris *n.*: disgrace, shame
dies, diei *m./f.*: a day
dignor (1): to deem, think worthy
fio, fieri (3): to happen, become
gloria, -ae *f.*: glory
grates, gratis *f.*: thanks
hostis, -is *m/f.*: an enemy
minimus -a -um: small, little

minor, -us: smaller
mora, -ae *f.*: a delay
nex, necis *f.*: death, murder
ops, opis *f.*: power
pendeo (2): to depend
pretium, preti(i) *n.*: price, value, worth
quantus, -a, -um: how great, how much
reddo (3): to return, give back
solus, -a, -um: only
spondeo: promise, pledge
tantus, -a, -um: of such size, so great
victor, victoris *m.*: a conqueror, victor
victoria, -ae *f.*: victory

---

dignetur: pres. subj. in future less vivid protasis, "*if* the lion *were to deem* the mouse *worthy*" + abl.

muri: dat. of possession, "be *the mouse's* glory"

coeperit: perf. subj. in future less vivid apodosis, "*would it not begin* to be?"

vincat: pres. subj. in present general protasis, "if (ever) he conquers"

vinci: pres. pass. inf. as pred., "to conquer so is *to be conquered*"

crimen habet: "to conquer *has a crime*" i.e. is a crime

sit ... sit: pres. subj. concessive, with infinitives as subjects, "*although to conquer is* an honor ... *although to conquer thus is* a praise"

minimo ... ab hoste: abl., "less *from a very small enemy*"

minus: pred., "would be *less*"

de pretio: "depends *on the value* of the conquered"

tantus erit .... quanta fuit: correlatives, "will be as great ... as was"

si ... possit: pres. subj. in future less vivid protasis, "if he could" + inf.

Nam leo rete subit nec prodest viribus uti,

    Sed prodest querulo murmure damna loqui.

Mus redit, hunc reperit, cernit loca, vincula rodit,

    Hac ope pensat opem; sic leo tutus abit.

Rem potuit tantam minimi prudentia dentis.

    Cui leo dans veniam se dedit ipse sibi.

Tu, qui summa potes, ne despice parva potentem:

    Nam prodesse potest, si quis obesse nequit.

---

cerno (3): to discern
damnum, damni *n.*: loss
dens, dentis *m.*: a tooth
despicio (3): to look down on
locum, -i *n.*: a position
loquor (3): to speak
murmur, -is *n.*: a roar
nequeo (4): to be unable to (+ *inf.*)
obsum, obesse: to hurt
penso (1): to compensate
prosum, prodesse: to be useful
prudentia, -ae *f.*: skillfulness

querulus, -a, -um: complaining
redeo, redire: return
reperio (4): to discover
rete, retis *n.*: a net
rodo (3): to gnaw
subeo, -ire: to enter
tutus, -a, -um : safe
utor (3): to use, make use of (+ *abl.*)
venia, -ae *f.*: favor, forgiveness
vinculum, -i *n.*: a chain, bond
vis, viris *f.*: strength

---

rete: abl. after *subit*, "he enters *a net*"
viribus: abl. after *uti*, "to use *his strength*"
querulo murmure: abl. of manner, "speaks *with a mournful roar*"
hac ope: abl. of means, "by this help"
potuit (sc. facere): "*was able* (to do)"
cui: "to whom" i.e. the mouse
dans: pres. part. instrumental, "by giving"
se ... ipse sibi : "*He himself* gave *himself to himself*" i.e. he helped himself
potentem: pres. part. acc., "despises *the one being capable of*"
si quis ... nequit: "if someone was unable to" i.e. if someone refrained from + inf.

Fable 19: De milvo egrotante

This fable relies on the reader understanding that, in this collection, the kite is a wicked animal. Here, a kite is dying, and asks for his last rights, but is denied them because he has been a criminal his entire life. The moral is rather religious, certainly not the kind of moral that would have been ascribed to an ancient fable. Here, appealing to the medieval sense of religion, the reader is reminded that repenting while dying is too late.

Morbi mole jacet milvus matremque precatur
Ut superis pro se det sacra detque preces.
Mater ait: "Mi nate, deos et sacra deorum
Laesisti; recolunt inpia facta dei.

---

aegroto (1): to be sick, be distressed
deus, **dei** *m.*: god
factum, **-i** *n.*: a fact, deed
inpius, **-a**, **-um**: wicked
jaceo (2): to lie, lie down
laedo, (**3**), **laesi**, **laesus**: to strike, hurt
mater, **matris** *f.*: a mother
milvus, **-i** *m.*: a kite, bird of prey
moles, **molis** *f.*: difficulty, weight

morbus, **-i** *m.*: sickness, illness
natus, **-i** *m.*: a son, child
precor (1): to beg
recolo (3): to remember
sacer, **-a**, **-um**: sacred, holy
sacrum, **sacri** *n.*: sacrifice, religious rites (pl.)
superum, **superi** *n.*: heaven (pl.), heavenly beings

---

jacet: "lies" i.e. is bed-ridden
ut ... det: pres. subj. noun clause after *precatur* , "begs her *to give*"
superis: dat., "give *to the gods*"

Criminis ultores pensant pro crimine poenam.

Cum sacra turbares, poena timenda fuit.

Te cogit timor esse pium, te poena fidelem;

Hic timor, haec pietas cum nece sera venit.

cogo (3): to restrict, confine	**poena, poenae** *f.*: a penalty, punishment
crimen, criminis *n.*: a crime	**serus, -a, -um**: late
fidelis, fidele: faithful, loyal	**timeo** (2): to fear, dread, be afraid
hirundo, hirundinis *f.*: a swallow	**timor, -is** *m.*: fear, dread
penso (1): to pay/punish for	**turbo** (1): to disturb, agitate
pietas, pietatis *f.*: responsibility, piety	**ultor, -is** *m.*: an avenger, revenger
pius, -a -um: pious, devout, holy	**venio** (4): to come

pro crimine: abl. of manner, "in return for the crime"

cum ... turbares: impf. subj. cum circumstantial, "*when you were disturbing* the holy things"

timenda fuit: gerundive in passive past periphrastic with contrafactual force, "punishment *ought to have been feared*"

pium ... fidelem: acc. pred., "compels you to be *pious...faithful*"

pietas ... sera: nom., "*this piety* comes *late*"

cum nece: abl. of attendant circumstance, "with a death"

Fable 20: De hirundine aves monente

In this fable a wise swallow warns the other birds that they should eat the flax seed when it is sown, so that the farmer will not use it to ensnare them later. The birds refuse to listen, so the swallow befriends the humans instead. Just as the swallow predicted, the other birds are ensnared after the flax is harvested, and the moral warns again rejecting wise council.

Ut linum pariat de lini semine, semen

   Nutrit humus, sed aves tangit hirundo metu:

"Hic ager, hoc semen nobis mala vincla minatur;

   Vellite pro nostris semina sparsa malis."

Turba fugit sanos monitus vanosque timores

   Arguit; exit humo semen et herba viret.

Rursus hirundo monet instare pericula; rident

   Rursus aves. Hominem placat hirundo sibi

---

ager, **agri** *m.*: a field, land
arguo (3): to denounce
avis, **avis** *f.*: a bird
exeo, **exire**: to come, emerge, sprout
fugio (3): to flee, fly
habito (1): to inhabit, dwell
herba, -ae *f.*: herb, grass
humus, -i *f.*: ground, soil
insto (1): to approach, threaten
linum, -i *n.*: flax
malus, -a, -um: evil, wicked
metus, **metus** *m.*: fear, anxiety
minor (1): to force, threaten
moneo (2): to remind, advise, warn
monitus, -us *m.*: warnings
nutrio (4): to nourish

pario (1): to acquire
periculum, -i *n.*: danger
placo (1): to reconcile X (*acc.*) with Y (*dat.*)
rideo (2): to laugh, ridicule
rursus: again
sanus, -a, -um: sound, healthy
semen, **seminis** *n.*: a seed
spargo (3) **sparsi**, **sparsum**: to scatter, sow (seeds)
tango (3): to touch, strike
turba, ae *f.*: a crowd, mob
vanus, -a, -um: empty, vain
vello: (3): to pluck, pull
vinclum, -i *n.*: a chain, bond
vir, **viri** *m.*: a man
vireo (2): to be green, be lively

---

ut pariat: pres. subj. in purpose clause, "*in order to aquire* the flax"
metu: abl. of means, "strikes *with fear*"
pro nostris ... malis: expressing purpose, "sown *for your harm*"
vanosque timores: acc. pred., "denounces them *as vain fears*"
humo: abl. of place from which, "sprouts *from the ground*"
instare: pres, inf, in ind. st., "warns *that dangers are approaching*"

45

Cumque viris habitans cantu blanditur amico:

Nam praevisa minus laedere tela solent.

Jam metitur linum, jam fiunt retia, jam vir

Fallit aves, jam se conscia culpat avis.

Utile consilium qui spernit, inutile sumit;

Qui nimis est tutus, retis jure subit.

amicus, -a, -um: friendly
blandior (4): to soothe
cantus, cantus *m.*: a song
conscius, -a, -um: knowing
consilium, -i *n.*: advice, counsel
culpo (1): to blame
fallo (3): to deceive, ensnare
fio, fieri: to happen, become
inutilis, -e: useless
jure: by right, rightly
laedo(3): to strike, hurt
linum, lini *n.*: flax

meto (3): to reap
minus: less
nimis: very much, too much
praevisus, -a, -um: foreseen
rete, -is *n.*: a net
soleo (2): to be in the habit of (+ *inf.*)
sperno (3): to scorn
subeo (4): go into , enter (+ *gen.*)
sumo (3): to take up
telum, -i *n.*: a dart, spear
utilis, utile: useful

cantu amico: abl. of means, "soothe *with friendly song*"
conscia avis: nom. subj., "the knowing bird(s)" singular for the whole flock

Fable 21: De Attica terra et rege

In some manuscripts these fables are split, 21a and 21b. In others they are presented as two entirely separate fables, and still others present them as one united fable. They are essentially two versions of the same story. The first, however, is told of the Athenians, who begged for a king until they were ruled by a tyrant. The human characters, and the setting of the fable in Athens makes this story feel rather unfabular, but at the end of the tale, we are told that Aesop tells a tale suitable to this situation. The resulting fable fits well with rest of the collection. Just as the Athenians, the frogs beg for a king. First Jupiter gives them a stick, but they are soon disenchanted with the inanimate king, and beg for another. The second time, Jupiter gives them a snake, who, of course, begins to eat them. The frogs then plead with Jupiter yet again, asking that he deliver them from the snake, but Jupiter only laughs, telling them that he has granted their wishes. The moral of both fables is given at the end, and reminds the reader to be happy with what they have.

Fabula, nata sequi mores et pingere vitam,

    Tangit quod fugias quodve sequaris iter.

Rege carens nec regis inops, sine lege nec exlex,

    Absque jugo gessit Attica terra jugum.

Libertas, errare negans, se sponte coegit

Atticus, -a, -um: Attic, Athenian	**libertas, libertatis** *f.*: freedom
careo: be without (+ *abl.*)	**mos, moris** *m.*: custom, habit
cogo (3) **coegi, coactus**: compel	**nascor** (3) **natus sum**: to be born, begotten
erro (1): to wander, err	**nego** (1): to refuse (+ *inf.*)
exlex, exlegis (*gen.*): lawless	**pingo** (3): to decorate, depict
fabula, fabulae *f.*: a story, fable	**rego** (3): to rule
fugio (3): to flee	**rex, regis** *m.*: a king
gero (3), **gessi**: bear, carry	**sequor** (3): to follow
inops, inopis (*gen.*): lacking (+ *gen.*)	**spons, spontis** *f.*: free will
iter, itineris *n.*: a journey	**tango** (3): to touch, influence
jugum, -i *n.*: a yoke	**terra, -ae** *f.*: earth, land
lex, legis *f.*: law	**vita, -ae** *f.*: life

---

sequi...et pingere: pres. inf. of purpose after *nata*, "born in order *to follow and depict*"

fugias ... sequaris: pres. subj. in indirect deliberative question, "what road *you should flee* ... or what road *you should follow*"

rege: abl. of separation after carens, "lacking *a king*"

absque jugo .... jugum: "*and without a (metaphorical) yoke* bore *a (literal) yoke*"

se sponte coegit: "freedom compelled itself willingly" a *paradox*

Et pudor ob legem fortior ense fuit.

Ne libitum faceret, regem plebs libera fecit

Et quae non potuit pellere jussa tulit.

Rex coepit lenire truces, punire nocentes,

Quaequae levanda levans, quaequae premenda premens.

Hos onerat novitas: cives in lege novelli,

Quod leviter possent, vix potuere pati.

Urbem triste jugum querula cervice ferentem

Aesopus tetigit, consona verba movens.

Aesopus, -i *m.*: Aesop
cervix, cervicis *f.*: a neck
civis, civis *m./f.*: a fellow citizen
coepio (3), **coepi**: begin (+ *inf.*)
consonus, -a, -um: harmonious
ensis, ensis *m.*: a sword
fero, ferre, tuli, latus: to bear
fortior, -us: stronger
jussum, -i *n.*: an order
lenio (4): to calm, placate
leviter: lightly
levo (1): to lift up, make smooth
liber, -a, -um: free, unconstrained
libet: it is pleasing
moveo (2): to move
nocens, nocentis (*gen.*): guilty, criminal

novellus, -a, -um: new, for the first time
novitas, novitatis *f.*: newness, novelty
onero (1): to oppress
patior (3): to suffer, endure
pello (3): to drive away
plebs, plebis *f.*: common people
premo (3): to pursue, oppress
pudor, -is *m.*: decency
punio (4): to punish
querulus, -a, -um: quarrelsome
tango (3), **tetigi**: touch
tristis, triste: sad
trux, trucis (*gen.*): wild
urbs, urbis *f.*: a city
verbum, -i *n.*: a word
vix: hardly

---

ob legem: "instead of law"

ense: abl. of comparison after *fortior*, "stronger *than a sword*"

ne faceret: imperf. subj. in negative purpose clause, "*lest it (i.e. plebs) do* whatever is pleasing"

libitum: supine acc. of *libet*, "lest he do *what is pleasing*"

quae: acc. neut. pl. with ancedent jussa,, "orders *which*"

levanda...premenda: gerundives acc. pl., "what ought to be raised up...what ought to be oppressed"

cives ... novelli: transferred epithet, "*citizens new* under the law" i.e. under a new law

possent: imperf. subj. in relative clause of characteristic, "that *which they could* have endured"

potuere: apocope (= *potuerunt*), "*they were able* scarcely" +inf.

pati: pres. dep. inf., "able *to endure*"

querula cervice: abl. of place, "on its quarrelsome neck"

(21b) Cum nihil auderet ludentes laedere ranas,

Supplicuere Jovi ne sine rege forent.

Jupiter huic voto risum dedit. Ausa secundas

Rana preces, subitum sensit in amne sonum.

Nam Jove dante trabem, trabis ictu flumine moto,

Demersit subitus guttura rauca timor.

Placato rediere metu, videre tigillum,

Stando procul regem pertimuere suum.

---

amnis, amnis *m.*: a river
audeo (2): to dare
demergo (3), **demersi**: submerge, plunge
flumen, fluminis *n.*: a river, stream
guttur, -is *n.*: a throat, neck
ictus, ictus *m.*: a blow
Jupiter, Jovis *m.*: Jupiter
laedo (3): to strike, hurt
ludo (3): to play, frolic
moveo (2) **movi, motus**: to set in motion
pertimesco (3), **pertimui**: become very scared (of)
placo (1): to appease, placate
prex, precis *f.*: a prayer, request
procul: at distance, far off

rana, -ae *f.*: a frog
raucus, -a, -um: hoarse
redeo, redire, redii, reditus: return
rego (3): to rule
risus, risus *m.*: laughter
secundus, -a, -um: following, second
sentio (4): to perceive, feel
sonus, -i *m.*: a noise, sound
subitus, -a, -um: sudden
supplico (1): to supplicate
tigillum, -i *n.*: a small beam
trabes, trabis *f.*: a tree-trunk, beam
video (2) **vidi**: see
votum, -i *n.*: a vow, wish

21b: see introductory note

cum auderet: imperf. subj. in cum circumstantial, "when nothing was daring"

supplicuere: perf. (= *supplicaverunt*), "they supplicated" + dat.

ne forent: imperf. subj. indirect command after *supplicuere*, "asked *not to be* without a king"

huic voto: dat. ind. obj., "gave a smile *to this wish*"

ausa: perf. part. dep. nom., "the frogs *having dared*"

Iove dante: abl. abs., "Jupiter giving"

ictu: abl. of means, "moved *by the blow*"

flumine moto: abl. abs., "the river having been moved"

demersit: perf., "fear *submerged* them" i.e. caused them all to punge underwater

placato metu: abl. abs., "their fear having been placated"

rediere: perf. (= *redierunt*), "they returned"

videre: perf. (= *viderunt*), "they saw"

stando: gerund abl. of *sto*, "*by standing* far away"

pertimuere: perf. (= *pertimuerunt*), "they feared"

Ut novere trabem per se non posse moveri,

Pro duce fecerunt tertia vota Jovi.

Ira Iovem movit, regem dedit, intulit hidrum.

Hidrus hiante gula coepit obire lacum.

Clamitat ecce lacus: "Morimur, pie Jupiter; audi,

Jupiter, exaudi! Jupiter, affer opem!

Nos sepelit venter, nostri sumus esca tyranni;

Aufer caedis opus, redde quietis opes."

Ille refert: "Emptum longa prece ferte magistrum.

Vindicet eternus otia spreta metus."

---

affero, afferre: to convey to, bring
audio (4): to hear
aufero, auferre: to convey away
caedes, caedis: murder
clamito (1): to cry out
coepio (3) **coepi**: begin (+ *inf.*)
dux, ducis *m.*: a leader
emo (3), **emi, emptus**: acquire, obtain
esca, -ae *f.*: food
eternus, -a -um: eternal, everlasting
exaudio (4): to hear clearly, comply with
gula, -ae *f.*: a throat
hidrus, -i *m.*: a water-serpent, snake
hio (1): to be wide open
infero (3) **intuli**: bring in, inflict
ira, -ae *f.*: anger
lacus, -us *n.*: a lake

longus, -a, -um: long, boundless
magister, magistri *m.*: a master
morior (3): to die
moveo (2) **movi**: move
nosco (3) **novi**: get to know
obeo (4): to set upon, approach
ops, opis *f.*: help
opus, operis *n.*: work
otium, -i *n.*: leisure
pius, -a, -um: holy
quiesco (3): to rest
reddo (3): to return
refero, referre: to answer
sepelo (3): to bury, submerge
tyrannus, -i *m.*: a tyrant
venter, ventris *m.*: a stomach
vindico (1): to punish, avenge

---

novere: (= *noverunt*), "they knew"
non posse: pres. inf. in ind. st. after *novere*, "realized that the beam *is not able*" +inf.
Iovi: dat. ind. obj., "made prayers *to Jupiter*"
hiante gula: abl. abs., "with his throat gaping"
lacus: metonymy for all of the frogs in the lake
esca: nom. pred., "we are *the food*"
caedis: gen. after *opus*, "help *from the slaughter*"
quietis: gen. after *opes*, "wealth *of rest*"
longa prece: abl. of means, "obtained *by long prayer*"
vindicet: pres. subj. jussive, "*let* eternal fear *avenge!*"

Omne boni pretium nimio vilescit in usu,

    Fitque, mali gustu, dulcius omne bonum.

Si quis habet quod habere decet, sit laetus habendo:

    Alterius non sit qui suus esse potest.

alter, -**a**, -**um**: one of two
bonus, -**i** *m.*: good
decet (2): to it is right (+ *inf.*)
dulcior, -**us**: more pleasant
fio, **fieri**: to happen, become
gustus, **gustus** *m.*: a tasting
habeo (2): to have

laetus, -**a**, -**um**: happy
malus, -**a** -**um**: bad, evil
nimius, -**a**, -**um**: excessive
omnis, **omne**: all
pretium, **preti(i)** *n.*: a price, value
usus, **usus** *m.*: use
vilesco (3): to become worthless

boni: gen. objective, "the value *of good*"
gustu: abl. of means, "*by the taste* of evil"
sit: pres. subj. jussive, "let him be happy"
habendo: gerund abl., "be happy *by having*"
alterius: gen. of *alter*, "of another"
non sit: pres. subj. jussive, "let him not be another's" where *ne* is normal
suus: nom. pred., "able to be *his own* (master)"

Fable 22: De accipitre et columbis

This fable continues the theme of the previous two; apparently a tyranical king is an issue that was particularly significant to the author of this collection. Here, it is the doves that accept a hawk as their king, hoping that he will help them ward off the attacks of the kite. Ultimately the hawk does more damage to the flock than the kite, and the moral encourages bearing lesser burdens (the kite) in order to avoid greater pain.

Accipitrem milvi pulsurum bella columbae

Accipiunt regem; rex magis hoste nocet.

Incipiunt de rege queri, quod sanius esset

Milvi bella pati quam sine Marte mori.

Si quid agis, prudenter agas et respice finem.

Ferre minora volo, ne graviora feram.

---

accipio (3): to take, accept
accipiter, accipitris *m./f.*: a hawk
ago (3): to do
bellum, -i *n.*: an attack
columba, -ae *f.*: a pigeon, dove
finis, finis *m./f.*: an end, outcome
gravior, -us: heavy, painful
hostis, -is *m/f.*: an enemy
incipio (3): to begin (+ *inf.*)
Mars, Martis *m.*: Mars

milvus, -i *m.*: a kite, bird of prey
minor, -us: small, little
noceo (2): to harm, hurt
patior (3): to suffer, allow
pello (3) pulsi, pulsus: beat, drive out
queror (3): to complain
respicio (3): to look back at, consider
sanus, -a, -um: sound, healthy
volo, velle: to wish (+ *inf.*)

---

pulsurum: fut. part. agreeing with *regem* and expressing purpose, "in order that he beat (the hawk) away"

regem: acc. pred., "they accept the hawk *as a king*"

hoste: abl. of comparison after *magis*, "he harms more than *the enemy*"

quod esset: impf. subj. in ind. st. after *queri*, "to complain *that it would be* healthier"

pati: inf. epexegetic after *sanius*, "healthier *to suffer*"

sine Marte: personification, "without war"

agas: pres. subj. jussive, "may you do wisely"

ne feram: pres. subj. in negative purpose clause, "*lest I bear* greater ones"

52

Fable 23: De fure et cane

In this fable it becomes clear that, in the world of the fables, humans are just another breed of animal, and they interact with the animal characters just as two animals would interact. Here, it is the animal that appears more virtuous and the human who is villainous. A thief tries to lure a dog with baited food, but the dog is wiser than the man, and bays loudly, chasing the man away. While it may seem shocking for humans to play a part in what are typically understood as animal tales, this is not the only occurence in this collection. The use of humans only solidifies the message that man's behavior isn't much better than that which is exemplified by the animals.

Fure vocante canem praetenso munere panis,

Spreto pane, movet talia verba canis:

"Ut sileam tua dona volunt furtisque laborant

Esse locum; panem si fero, cuncta feres.

Fert munus mea damna tuum, latet hamus in esca:

Me privare cibo cogitat iste cibus.

---

canis, canis *m/f.*: a dog, hound
cibus, -i *m.*: food
cogito (1): to think, intend (+ *inf.*)
cunctus, -a, -um: all, whole
damnum, -i *n.*: loss, injury
donum, -i *n.*: a gift, present
fur, furis *m./f.*: a thief, robber
furtum, -i *n.*: theft, trick
hamus, -i *m.*: a hook
laboro (1): to work, accomplish
lateo (2): to lie hidden

locum, -i *n.*: a place, opportunity
munus, muneris *n.*: service, gift
panis, panis *m.*: bread
praetendo (3), **praetendi, praetensus**: extend, offer
privo (1): to deprive, rob
sileo (2): to be silent
sperno (3) **sprevi, spretus**: to scorn, despise
talis, -e: such, so great
verbum, -i *n.*: a word
voco (1): to call, summon

---

fure vocante: abl. abs., "the robber calling"
praetenso munere: abl. abs., "gift having been extended"
spreto pane: abl. abs., "the bread having been despised"
sileam: pres. subj. volative clause after *volo*, "wish *that I be silent*"
furtis: dat. after *locum*, " opportunity *for thefts*"
esse: pres. inf. in noun clause after *laborant*, "labor *that there be* an opportunity"
cibo: abl. of separation, "deprived *of food*"

Non amo nocturnum panem plus pane diurno,

    Advena plus noto non placet hostis hero.

Non rapiet nox una mihi bona mille dierum:

    Nolo semper egens esse semelque satur.

Latratu tua furta loquar, nisi sponte recedas."

    Hic silet, ille manet; hic tonat, ille fugit.

Si tibi quid detur, cur detur respice; si des,

    Cui des, ipse nota; teque, gulose, doma.

---

advena, -ae *m./f.*: a foreigner
amo (1): to love
dies, diei *m./f.*: day
diurnus, -a, -um: by day, daily
domo (1): to master, conquer
egens -ntis (*gen.*): needy, poor
fugio (3): to flee
gulosus, -a, -um: gluttonous
herus, -i *m.*: a master
latro (1): to bark, bark at
loquor (3): to speak, tell
maneo (2): to remain, stay
mille: thousand
nocturnus, -a, -um: nocturnal, of night

nolo, nolle: to be unwilling (+ *inf.*)
noto (1): to take note of
notus, -a, -um: known
nox, noctis *f.*: night
placeo (2): to please, satisfy
rapio (3): to drag off, seize
recedo (3): to recede, leave
satur, -a, -um: well-fed, rich
semel: one time
semper: always
spons, spontis *f.*: free will
tono (1): to thunder
unus, -a, -um: alone

---

pane diurno: abl. of comparison, "more than *bread of the day*"
noto hero: abl. of comparison, "more than a known friend"
advena hostis: "a foreign enemy" two nouns instead of noun+adj., an example of *hendiadys*
latratu: abl. supine, "tell *with barking*"
recedas: pres. subj. future less vivid apodosis, "unless *you recede*"
sponte: abl. of manner, "leave *by free will*"
si...detur: pres. subj. in pres. general condition, "if something is given to you"
cur detur: pres. subj. in indirect question, "consider *why it is given*"
si des: pres. subj, in pres. general condition, "if you give"
cui des: pres. subj. in indirect question, "take note *to whom you give*"

Fable 24: De lupo et sue

Echoing the message of the previous fable, the fable of the pig and the wolf is one of the few where an animal behaves wisely, and is able to save herself through this wisdom. A wolf attempts to convince a pig to let him watch over her newly born litter so that she might rest. The pig sees through this ploy and sends the wolf away, and the moral emphasizes that the cautious behavior of the pig is one the reader should emulate.

Vult lupus ut pariat maturum sucula fetum,

Seque novi curam spondet habere gregis.

Sus ait: "Hac cur careas, mihi nolo ministres.

Horrent obsequium viscera nostra tuum.

I procul, ut tutos liceat mihi fundere fetus.

I procul, et pietas haec erit apta mihi.

---

aptus, -a -um: suitable to (+ *dat.*)
careo (2): to be without, miss (+ *abl.*)
cur: why?
cura, -ae *f.*: concern, care
eo, ire: to go, walk
fetus, fetus *m.*: offspring, young
fundo (3): to pour, deliver
grex, gregis *m./f.*: a litter, herd
horreo (2): to dread, shrink from
licet (2): to it is permitted, one may
lupus, -i *m.*: a wolf
maturus, -a, -um: early, mature

ministro (1): to attend (to), serve
novus, -a -um: new, young
obsequium, -i *n.*: compliance, obedience
pario (3): to bear, give birth to
pietas, pietatis *f.*: responsibility, loyalty
procul: away, at distance
spondeo (2): promise, give pledge
sucula, -ae *f.*: a little pig
sus, suis *m./f.*: a swine, pig
tutus, -a -um: safe, secure
viscus, visceris *n.*: innards

---

ut pariat: pres. subj. in noun clause object of *vult*, "wishes *that she* (i.e. the sucula) *would give birth*"

se habere: indirect statement after *spondet*, "he pledges *that he has*"

novi gregis: obj. gen. after *curam*, "care *of the new litter*"

careas: pres. subj. deliberative, "why *would you miss* this?" i.e. why *would you want* this?

hac: abl. of separation after *careas*, referring to *curam*

ministro: pres subj in noun clause after *nolo*, "I do not wish *that you serve*"

ut liceat: pres. subj. in purpose clause, "go *so that it is permitted*" +inf.

mihi: dat. after *apta*, "suitable *to me*"

timuisse: perf. inf. in ind. com., "orders a parent *to fear*"

Pro natis natura jubet timuisse parentem."

Fine dato verbis hic abit, illa parit.

Tempore non omni non omnibus omnia credas:

Qui misere credit, creditur esse miser.

abeo: depart, go away	**natura, -ae** *f.*: nature
credo (3): to trust, entrust	**natus, -i** *m.*: a son, child
do (1) **dedi, datus**: give	**parens, parentis** *m./f.*: a parent
finis, finis *m./f.*: a boundary, end	**tempus, temporis** *n.*: time
jubeo (2): to order, command (+ *inf.*)	**timeo** (2) **timui**: fear, dread
miser, -a, -um: poor, miserable	

fine dato: abl. absolute, "*an end having been given* to the words"

non omni non omnibus omnia: *not every* time should you trust *all to not all*" i.e. to anyone. note the elaborate litotes and the acoustic impact of the words and their order

credas: pres. subj. in jussive clause, "you should trust"

misere: adv., "who trusts *miserably*" i.e. who trusts too much

misere … miser: note the *figura etymologica*

Fable 25: De terra parturiente murem

This is another fable which provides a ridiculous image, something which also seems to have aided its medieval popularity. The earth is swollen, and continues to swell, which frightens many people. Finally the swollen earth gives birth to a mouse, and the fear gives way to laughter because of the small size of the mouse. The moral continues to poke fun, saying that those who claim great things often do less. The cast of characters in this fable is quite unusual; much like the earlier fable about the sun wishing to wed, here both planets and animals are animated, and the fable also has human characters. The animated planets don't necessarily have the same humbling effect as the humanized animals; it isn't as easy to look at the planets and see a reflection of human behavior. Instead, perhaps these planets are a carry-over from the ancient fables, and serve effectively to indicate great size, even to a medieval audience. It must have been difficult for the illustrator to conceive what a planet might look like, so it seems a rock is used in the woodcut instead.

Terra tumet; tumor ille gemit gemituque fatetur

Partum: paene perit sexus uterque metu.

Cum tumeat tellus, monstrat se monstra daturam;

Dicunt et trepidant et prope stare cavent.

---

caveo (2): to take precautions not to (+ *inf.*)
dico (3): to say, state, allege
fateor (2): to admit, bespeaks
gemitus, gemitus *m.*: a groan
gemo (3): to moan, groan
metus, metus *m.*: fear, anxiety
monstro (1): to show, point out
monstrum, -i *n.*: a monster
mus, muris *m./f.*: a mouse
paene: almost
parturio (4): to be in labor, bring forth

partus, -us *m.*: a giving birth
pereo (4): to die, pass away
prope: near, nearly, close by, almost
sexus, sexus *m.*: sex, gender
sto (1): to stand
tellus, telluris *f.*: earth
terra, -ae *f.*: earth
trepido (1): to tremble, be afraid
tumeo (2): to swell, become inflated
tumor, tumoris *m.*: a swelling
uterque: each of two

---

metu: abl. of cause, "perishes *from fear*"

tumeat: pres. subj. in *cum* causal clause, "since the earth was swollen"

se daturam (sc. esse): fut. inf. in ind. st. after *monstrat*, "shows *that she is about to give*"

57

In risum timor ille redit: nam turgida murem

    Terra parit; jocus est quod timor ante fuit.

Saepe minus faciunt homines qui magna minantur.

    Saepe gerit nimios causa pusilla metus.

ante: (*adv.*) before	**nimius**, **-a**, **-um**: excessive, too great
causa, **-ae** *f.*: a cause	**pario** (3): to bear, give birth to
gero (3): to bear	**pusillus**, **-a** **-um**: tiny, very small
homo, **hominis** *m.*: a man, human being	**redeo**, **redire**: return
jocus, **-i** *m.*: a joke	**risus**, **risus** *m.*: laughter
magnus, **-a**, **-um**: large/	**timor**, **-is** *m.*: fear, dread
minor (1): to threaten	**turgidus**, **-a**, **-um**: swollen
minor, **minus**: less	

Fable 26: De agno et lupo

There are a number of fables in the elegiac Romulus that feature a wolf and a lamb; in this one, a lamb has been raised by a surrogate mother, a goat. The wolf is trying to cause discord, and asks why the lamb doesn't find her own mother, but the lamb cannot be shaken, saying that the goat has always provided her with all she needs. The lamb also acknowledges that she has grown much stronger nourished by the goat's milk, and it is important that she grow as much fleece as possible for her master. The moral notes that nothing is worse than a wicked warning and evil counsel, which the wolf tried to provide. The lamb's comment about the worth of her fleece is one of a few moments in this collection where the fables are grounded more pragmatically in the medieval world, and it breeches the divide that usually exists between the world of the fables and the realities of medieval life. Moments like these in the fables open the door for later fable collections which bring elements of social and political life into the fables.

Cum grege barbato dum ludit junior agnus,

Tendit in hunc menti dissona verba lupus:

"Cur olidam munda sequeris plus matre capellam?

Lac tibi preberet dulcius ipsa parens;

---

agnus, -i *m.*: a lamb
barbatus, -a, -um: bearded, (as sign of) adult
capella, -ae *f.*: a she-goat
dissonus, -a, -um: dissonant, different
dulcior, -us: pleasant, charming
grex, gregis *m.*: a flock, herd
junior, junius: younger
lac, lactis *n.*: milk
ludo (3): to play

lupus, -i *m.*: a wolf
mater, matris *f.*: a mother
mens, mentis *f.*: mind, intention
mundus, -a, -um: clean
olidus, -a, -um: stinking
parens, parentis *m./f.*: a parent
prebeo (2): to present, offer
sequor (3): to follow
tendo (3): to extend

---

barbato: "with the *bearded* flock" i.e. goats
tendit verba: "extends words" i.e. speaks
in hunc: "directs *against him*" i.e. the lamb
menti dissona: abl. of means, "with a dissonant mind" i.e. a troublesome intention
munda matre: abl. of comparison after *plus*, "more than *your clean mother*"
preberet: imperf. subj. in present contrafactual apodosis with protasis suppressed, "your own mother *would provide*" i.e. if she were here

59

Est prope, festina, matrem pete, munera matris,

    Lac bibe: nam servat ubera plena tibi."

Agnus ad haec: "Pia capra mihi lac dulce propinat,

    Me vice matris alit, me vice matris amat.

Non mihi, sed domino prodest me vivere: vivo

    Ut metat in tergo vellera multa meo.

Ergo mihi praestat nutriri lacte caprino

    Quam, lac matris habens, mergar in ore tuo."

---

alo (3): to feed
bibo (3): to drink
capra, -ae *f.*: a she-goat, nanny-goat
caprinus, -a, -um: of goats
dominus, -i *m.*: an owner, lord
dulcis, dulce: pleasant, sweet
festino (1): to hasten, hurry
habeo (2): to have
lacte, lactis *n.*: milk
mater, matris *f.*: a mother
mergo (3): to dip, plunge
meto (3): to reap, cut off
munus, muneris *n.*: a gift
nutrio (4): to suckle

os, oris *n.*: a mouth
peto (3): to desire, beg
pius, -a -um: affectionate, tender, devout
praesto (1): to be better (+ *inf.*)
prope: near
propino (1): to give to drink
prosum, prodesse: be useful to (+ *dat.*)
servo (1): to preserve X (*acc.*) for Y (*dat.*)
tergum, -i *n.*: a back
uber, uberis *n.*: an udder
vellus, velleris *n.*: fleece
vicis, vicis *f.*: a turn, change
vivo (3): to live

---

lac: in apposition to *munera*, "drink *milk*, the gifts of your mother"
vice: abl., "in place of" + gen.
vivere: pres. inf. complementary after *prodest*, "profits me *to live*"
metat: pres. subj. in purpose clause, "I live *in order that he reap*"
lacte caprino: abl. of means, "nurtured *with goat milk*"
habens: pres. part. concessive, "my mother *although having* milk"
mergar: pres. subj. in noun clause after *quam*, "rather than *that I be plunged*"

Omnes vincit opes securam ducere vitam.

Pauperius nihil est quam miser usus opum.

Nil melius sano monitu, nil pejus iniquo:

Consilium sequitur certa ruina malum.

certus, -a, -um: certain	**pauper, -a, -um**: poor
consilium, -i *n.*: debate	**pejor, -us**: worse
duco (3): to lead	**ruina, -ae** *f.*: a fall
iniquus, -a, -um: hostile	**sanus, -a, -um**: sound
melior, -us: better	**securus, -a, -um**: secure
miser, -a, -um: poor, miserable	**usus, usus** *m.*: use
monitus, monitus *m.*: warning, advice	**vinco** (3): to conquer
ops, opis *f.*: power, wealth	**vita, -ae** *f.*: life

ducere: pres. inf. subject of vincit, "*to lead* a secure life conquers"
sano monitu: abl. of comparison after *melius*, "better than *sound advice*"
iniquo: abl. of comparison after peius, "worse than hostile advice"

Fable 27: De cane vetulo

In this fable, an elderly dog is less apt at hunting than he once was. His master is upset and lashes out at the dog, who reminds the master of his prowess in younger years. Rather than punish the master for his unfaithful anger, however, the moral broadens to assert that love is contingent upon the giving of gifts. Once the gifts cease, the love often ends. The last two lines broaden once more to a political point: whoever serves an unjust man is destined to serve in misery.

Armavit natura canem pede, dente, juventa:

Hinc levis, hinc mordax, fortis et inde fuit.

Tot bona furatur senium: nam robore privat

Corpus, dente genas, et levitate pedes.

Hic leporem prendit, fauces lepus exit inermes.

Elumbem domini verberat ira canem.

---

armo (1): to equip
canis, canis *m/f.*: a dog, hound
corpus, corporis *n.*: a body
dens, dentis *m.*: a tooth
elumbis, elumbe: weak, feeble
exeo, exire: to come, go
faux, faucis *f.*: a mouth
fortis, forte: strong
furor (1): to steal, plunder
gena, -ae *f.*: cheeks
inde: thence
inermis, inerme: unarmed, toothless
ira, -ae *f.*: anger
juventa, -ae *f.*: youth

lepus, leporis *m.*: a hare
levis, leve: light
levitas, levitatis *f.*: lightness
mordax, -acis (*gen.*): biting, snappish
natura, -ae *f.*: nature
pes, pedis *m.*: a foot
prendo (3): to catch, catch up with
privo (1): to deprive, rob
robus, roboris *n.*: strength, firmness
senium, -i *n.*: condition of old age
tot: so many
verbero (1): to beat, strike
vetulus, -a, -um: elderly, aging

---

pede, dente, juventa: abl. of means, "armed with *feet, teeth, youth*"
hinc...hinc ... inde: from the first, from the second, from the third"
robore, dente, levitate: abl. of separation after privat, "old age separates *from his strength, his teeth, his lightness*"
hic: i.e. the young dog
fauces inermes: "the toothless mouth" i.e. of the old dog

Reddit verba canis: "Dum me pia pertulit aetas,

    Nulla meum potuit fallere praeda pedem.

Defendit senii culpam laus ampla juventae;

    Pro sene qui cecidit, facta priora vigent.

Nullus amor durat nisi fructus servet amorem:

    Quilibet est tanti munera quanta facit.

Magnus eram, dum magna dedi: nunc marcidus annis

    Vileo, de veteri mentio nulla bono.

---

aetas, aetatis *f.*: lifetime, age
amor, amoris *m.*: love
amplus, -a, -um: great, large
annus, -i *m.*: a year
bonus, -a -um: good, honest
cado (3) **cecidi**: to fall
culpa, -ae *f.*: fault, blame
defendo (3): to defend
duro (1): to harden
factum, facti *n.*: fact, deed, act, achievement
fallo (3): to deceive, slip by
fructus, fructus *m.*: produce, crops
laus, laudis *f.*: praise
magnus, -a -um: large, great
marcidus, -a, -um: withered

mentio, mentionis *f.*: mention
munus, muneris *n.*: service, gift
nullus, -a, -um: no, none
perfero (3) **pertuli**: carry through, endure
pius, -a, -um: tender, devoted
praeda, -ae *f.*: prey
prior, prius: previous, earlier
quantus, -a, -um: how great, how much
quilibet: someone
reddo (3): to return
senex, senis (*gen.*): aged, old
tantus, -a, -um: so great
vetus, veteris (*gen.*): old
vigeo (2): to be strong
vileo (2): to become worthless

---

servet: pres subj. in future less vivid protasis, "unless the result *keeps* the love"
tanti: gen. of value, "something is of *so much* value"
annis: abl. of specification, "withered *by the years*"
de veteri bono: "concerning my old good" i.e. prior service

Si laudas quod eram, quod sum culpare protervum est.

Si juvenem recipis, pellere turpe senem est."

Se misere servire sciat, qui servit iniquo.

Parcere subjectis nescit iniquus homo.

culpo (1): to blame
juvenis, juvenis *m./f.*: a youth
laudo (1): to recommend, praise
misere: wretchedly, desperately
nescio (4): to not know how to (+ *inf.*)
parco (3): to refrain from, spare (+ *dat.*)
pello (3): to beat, drive out

protervus, -a, -um: violent, reckless
recipio (3): to accept
scio (4): to know, understand
servio (4): to serve
subjectus, -i *m.*: a subject
turpis, -e: ugly, nasty

culpare: inf. epexegetic after *protervum*, "it is perverse *to blame*"
juvenem ... senem: predicates of *me* understood, "if you receive me *as a youth ... an old man*'"
se servire: ind. st. after *sciat*, "knows *that he serves*"
sciat: pres. subj. jussive clause, "let him know"
iniquo: dat. after *servit*, "who serves an *unjust* master"
subjectis: dat. after *parcere*, "to spare his *subjects*"

Fable 28: De leporibus et ranis

Here the animals and action in the fable are secondary to the moral (and religious) lesson that is being taught. A group of hares is frightened by a noise in the forest, but their only means of escape is to dive into a pond which lies ahead of them. The hares see that there are also frogs in the water, and they decide to embrace hope, and dive into the water. The fable ends here, and the remaining eight lines are devoted to discussing the virtue of hope, and how it can serve as a remedy for fear. Not only is this message of hope rather than moral living a bit unusual, but this fable also fails to address the fate of the rabbits, who we are left to assume are able to swim across the pond (apparently rabbits, actually, are quite the swimmers).

Silva sonat, fugiunt lepores; palus obviat, haerent.

Fit mora: respiciunt ante retroque, timent.

Dum librant in mente metus, se mergere pacti,

Se metui et ranas stagna subire vident.

Unus ait: "Sperare licet; non sola timoris

Turba sumus: vano rana timore latet.

---

ante: forwards
fio, fieri: to happen, be made
fugio (3): to flee
haereo (2): to hesitate
lateo (2): to lie hidden
lepus, leporis *m.*: a hare
libro (1): to balance
licet (2): to it is permitted, one may (+ *inf.*)
mens, mentis *f.*: mind
mergo (3): to drown, submerge
metus, -us *m.*: fear
mora, -ae *f.*: a delay
obvio (1): to meet, be in the way
pacisco (3) **pactus sum**: to decide
palus, paludis *f.*: a swamp, marsh

rana, -ae *f.*: a frog
respicio (3): to look back at, gaze at
retro: backwards
silva, -ae *f.*: wood, forest
solus, -a, -um: only
sono (1): to make a sound
spero (1): to hope for, trust
stagnum, -i *n.*: a pool, lake
subeo, subire: to go under, undergo
timeo (2): to fear
timor, timoris *m.*: fear, dread
turba, -ae *f.*: a crowd
unus, -a, -um: one
vanus, -a, -um: empty, vain

---

mergere: pres. inf. in ind. st. after pacti, "having decided *to submerge* themselves"

subire: zeugma, construed with both *metui* and *stagna*, "they see themselves *to undergo* fear and they see the frogs *to go under* the water"

turba: nom. pred., "we are not the only *crowd*"

vano timore: abl. of manner, "hides with empty fear," i.e. empty of fear with transferred epithet

Spem decet amplecti, spes est via prima salutis.

    Saepe facit metui non metuenda metus.

Corporis est levitas et mentis inertia nobis:

    Ista fugae causam suggerit, illa fugam."

Sic timeat quicumque timet ne mole timoris

    Spe careat: gravis est spe fugiente timor.

Speret qui metuit: morituros vivere vidi

    Spe duce, victuros spe moriente mori.

---

amplector (3): to embrace
careo (2): to be without (+ *abl.*)
causa, -ae *f.*: a cause
decet (2): to it is fitting (+ *inf.*)
dux, ducis *m.*: a leader
fuga, -ae *f.*: a flight, fleeing
gravis, grave: heavy
inertia, -ae *f.*: sluggishness
levitas, -tatis *f.*: lightness
metuo (3) **metui**: fear

moles, molis *f.*: a mass
morior (3): to die
primus, -a, -um: first
salus, salutis *f.*: safety
spero (1): to hope for
spes, spei *f.*: hope
suggero (3): to suggest
via, -ae *f.*: a way
vinco (3) **vici, victus**: to conquer
vivo (3): to be alive, live

---

amplecti: pres. inf. dep. after *decet*, "it is fitting *to embrace*"

via prima: pred. nom., "hope is *the first way*"

metui: pres. pass. inf. after facit, "causes *to be feared*"

metuenda: gerundive, neut. pl. acc. obj. of *facit* and subject of inf. *metui*, "causes *things that ought not be feared* to be feared"

metus: subject of facit

ista ... illa: "the latter (*inertia*) ... the former (*levitas*)"

timeat: pres subj. jussive, "let him fear!"

quicumque timet: relative clause subject of *timeat*, "let *whoever fears* fear!" note the mannered variations on the words for fear and hope

mole: abl. of cause, "*because of the mass* of fear"

spe: abl. of separation, "lack *hope*"

ne careat: pres subj. negative purpose clause, "*lest he lack* hope"

spe fugiente: abl. abs., "with hope fleeing" Note the anaphora

speret: pres subj. jussive, "let him hope!"

morituros: fut. part. dep. acc. subject of *vivere* in ind. st. after *vidi*, "I have seen *those about to die* to live"

spe duce: abl. abs., "with hope being the leader"

victuros: fut. part. acc. subject of *mori* in ind. st. after *vidi*,, "I have seen *those about to win* to die"

spe moriente: abl. abs., "with hope dying"

Fable 29: De lupo et haedo

A source for one of the most popular fable tropes, the wolf in sheep's clothing, "The Kid and the Wolf" tells of a wolf who tries to deceive a kid by speaking with a goat's voice while her mother is away. The kid, however, forewarned of this kind of danger by his mother, is wise enough to see through the disguise, and he turns the wolf away. The moral praises the kid for listening to his parent. This fable is later combined with the Biblical metaphor of a wolf in sheep's clothing (*Matthew* 7:15), to form the popular fable of a wolf dressed as a sheep. Henryson tells a similar fable, although in reverse, where it is a sheep that dresses as a dog, in an attempt to protect his flock. Edmund Spenser is one of the first to present a wolf in sheep's clothing as a part of a fable, in his *Shepheardes Calender*.

Capra, cibum quaerens, haedum commendat ovili;

Hunc illic solida servat ovile sera.

Natum cauta parens monitu praemunit amico,

Ut lateat, nec sit in sua damna vagus.

---

amicus, -a, -um: friendly
capra, -ae *f*.: a she-goat, nanny-goat
cautus, -a, -um: cautious
cibus, -i *m*.: food
commendo (1): to entrust X (*acc.*) to Y (*dat.*)
damnum, -i *n*.: damage
haedus, -i *m*.: a kid, young goat
illic: there
lupus, -i *m*.: a wolf
monitus, monitus *m*.: a warning

natus, -i *m*.: a child
ovile, ovilis *n*.: a sheepfold
parens, parentis *m./f*.: a parent
praemunio (4): to fortify, forewarn
quaero (3): to seek
sera, -ae *f*.: a bar (for fastening doors)
servo (1): to watch over, protect
solidus, -a -um: solid
vagus, -a, -um: wandering

---

ovili: dat. after *commendat*, "entrusts *to the sheepfold*"
solida sera: abl. of means, "keeps *with a solid bar*"
monitu amico: abl. of means, "forewarns *with friendly advice*"
ut lateat: pres. subj. in ind. com. after *praemunit*, "warns *to lie hidden*"
nec sit: pres. subj. in negative purpose clause, "*lest he be* wandering into danger"

Hic latet; ecce lupus movet ostia, voce capellam

Exprimit, ut pateant hostia clausa petit.

"Sta procul," haedus ait, "Caprizas gutture falso;

Cum male caprizes, te procul esse volo.

Quod mea sis mater, mentitur imago loquendi.

Rimula, qua video, te docet esse lupum."

Insita natorum cordi doctrina parentum

Cum pariat fructum, spreta nocere solet.

---

capella, -ae *f.*: a she-goat
caprizo (1): to pretend to be a goat
clausus, -a, -um: shut/locked in, enclosed
cors, cordis *n.*: a heart
doceo (2): to show (+ *inf.*)
doctrina, -ae *f.*: education, learning
ecce: see! look!
exprimo (3): to imitate, copy
falsus, -a, -um: wrong, lying
fructus, fructus *m.*: produce, crops
guttur, -uris *n*: throat, neck
hostia, hostiorum *n.*: an enemy
imago, imaginis *f.*: a likeness
insitus, -a, -um: inserted, incorporated
lateo (2): to lie hidden

mater, matris *f.*: a mother
mentior (4): to lie, deceive
moveo (2): to move
natus, nati *m.*: a son, child
noceo (2): to harm, hurt
ostium, -i *n.*: a doorway, gate
pario (3): to bear, give birth to
pateo (2): to stand open, be open
peto (3): to attack
procul: at distance, far off
rimula, -ae *f.*: a small opening
soleo (2): to be in the habit of (+ *inf.*)
sperno (3) **sprevi, spretus**: to scorn, despise
volo, velle: to wish, want (+ *inf.*)
vox, vocis *f.*: a voice, tone, expression

---

hostia clausa: nom. pl., "that the *closed enemies* open" i.e. the doors
ut pateant: pres. subj. in noun clause after *petit*, "he seeks *that they open*"
gutture falso: abl. of means, "pretend *with a lying throat*"
cum caprizes: pres. subj. in causal clause, "*since you pretend* it badly"
quod sis: pres. subj. in noun clause after *mentitur*, "lie *that you are* my mother"
loquendi: gerund, gen., "likeness *of speaking*"
cordi: dat. after *insita*, "incorporated *into the heart*"
pariat: pres. subj. in cum circumstantial clause, "when *it produces* fruit"
spreta: perf. part. nom., "the teaching *having been despised*"

Fable 30: De rustico et angue

This fable has the opposite theme of the earlier serpent fable, "The Man and the Snake." The man and the snake dine together peacefully for many years, until the man becomes suddenly angered and strikes the snake. The man, overcome with remorse, begs forgiveness of the serpent. Because the man seems genuine in his sorrow, the animal forgives him. The moral, however, argues that this was irrational, and cautions that those who harm once are certain to harm again. The last line even states that the "honey" which comes from the mouth of a faithless man should be considered poison instead. This moral seemingly contradicts the Biblical lesson of turning the other cheek, and the role reversal is also particularly odd, as serpents are typically depicted as evil in the Middle Ages because of their association with the devil.

Rustica mensa diu nutritum noverat anguem;

Humanam potuit anguis amare manum.

Gratia longa viri subitam mutatur in iram;

Ira per anguineum dirigit arma caput.

Vulneris auctor eget, se vulnere credit egenum,

Angui pro venia supplicat; anguis ait:

---

amo (1): to love
anguineus, **-a**, **-um**: of a snake
anguis, **anguis** *m./f.*: a snake
arma, **armorum** *n.*: weapons
auctor, **auctoris** *m./f.*: an originator
caput, **capitis** *n.*: a head, person
credo (3): to trust
dirigo (3): to aim, direct
egenus, **-i** *m.*: a poor man
egeo (2): to be in need, poor
gratia, **-ae** *f.*: goodwill
humanus, **-a -um**: human
ira, **-ae** *f.*: anger
longus, **-a**, **-um**: long

manus, **manus** *f.*: a hand
mensa, **-ae** *f.*: a table
muto (1): to move
nosco (3) **novi**, **notum**: get to know, become acquainted
nutrio (4) **nutrivi**, **nutritum**: nourish, feed
rusticus, **-a**, **-um**: country
rusticus, **-i** *m.*: a peasant, farmer
subitus, **-a**, **-um**: sudden, rash
supplico (1): to pray, supplicate (+ *dat.*)
venia, **-ae** *f.*: favor, kindness
vir, **-i** *m.*: a man
vulnus, **vulneris** *n.*: a wound

---

nutritum: perf. part., "a serpent *having been nourished* a long time"
subitam in iram: into a sudden wrath" i.e. suddenly changed to wrath, transferred epithet
vulnere: abl. of cause, "believes *because of the wound*"
egenum: acc. pred. after *credit*, "he believes himself to be *a poor man*"

"Non ero securus, dum sit tibi tanta securis,

    Dum cutis haec memoret vulnera scripta sibi:

Qui me laesit, item laedet, si laedere possit.

    Expedit infido non iterare fidem.

Sed, si te piguit sceleris, scelus omne remitto:

    Nam gemitus veniam vulnere cordis emit."

Qui primo nocuit, vult posse nocere secundo;

    Quae dedit infidus, mella venena puto.

---

cor, cordis *n.*: a heart	**omnis, omne**: every, all
cutis, cutis *f.*: skin	**pigeo** (2) **pigui**: to displease, annoy
emo (3): to acquire, obtain	**primus, -a, -um**: first
expedio (4): to be expedient	**puto** (1): to think, consider
fides, fidei *f.*: faith	**remitto** (3): to send back, remit
gemitus, gemitus *m.*: a groan, sorrow	**scelus, sceleris** *n.*: crime
infidus, -a, -um: false	**scribo** (3) **scripsi, scriptum**: write
item: (*adv.*) likewise, further	**secundus, -a -um, second**
itero (1): to do a second time, repeat	**securis, securis** *f.*: an ax
laedo (3) **laesi**: strike	**securus, -a, -um**: secure, safe
mel, mellis *n.*: honey	**venenum, -i** *n.*: poison, drug
memoro (1): to remember	**venia, -ae** *f.*: favor
noceo (2), **nocui**: to harm	**vulnero** (1): to wound

securus ... securis: both nom., note the pun

dum sit: pres. subj. in proviso clause, "*so long as these is so great an ax*"

dum...memoret: pres. subj. in proviso clause, "*as long as* this skin *remembers*"

scripta: perf. part., "wounds *written* on it"

si posset: pres. subj. in future less vivid protasis, "if he should be able"

infido: dat. after iterare, "to repeat faith to *a false one*"

si piguit: impersonal, "*if there was annoyance* of the crime to you" i.e. if the crime annoyed you

vulnere: abl. of source, "sorrow *from a wound*"

primo ... secundo: "in the first place ... in the second place"

venena: acc. pred., "I consider the honey to be *poison*"

Fable 31: De cervo et ove et lupo

In this fable an agreement is made between a stag and a sheep that the sheep will repay a jar full of wheat which she owes. However, a wolf is present when the agreement is made, and after the wolf is gone, the sheep refuses to make the payment. The stag alone cannot incite enough fear to convince the sheep to repay, and he is forced to realize that it was only the presence of the wolf that intimidated the sheep. The moral warns against any agreement which is made in fear.

> Cervus ovi, presente lupo, sic intonat: "Amplum
>
> Vas tritici debes reddere, redde mihi."
>
> Sic jubet esse lupus, paret timor ista jubenti:
>
> Namque die fixo debita spondet ovis.
>
> Fit mora; cervus ovem vexat de foedere. Cervo
>
> Inquit ovis: "Non stant foedera facta metu.

---

amplus, -a, -um: great, large
cervus, -i *m.*: a stag, deer
debeo (2): to ought, must (+ *inf.*)
debitum, -i *n.*: debt
dies, diei *m./f.*: day
facio (3) **feci, factus**: do, make
figo (3) **fixi, fixus**: fasten, fix
fio, fieri: to happen, be made
foedus, foederis *n.*: a treaty
intono (1): to thunder, speak loudly
jubeo (2): to order, command (+ *inf.*)
lupus, -i *m.*: a wolf

metus, metus *m.*: fear
mora, -ae *f.*: a delay
ovis, ovis *f.*: a sheep
pareo (2): to obey (+ *dat.*)
praesum, -esse: to be present
reddo (3): to return
spondeo (2): to promises
sto (1): to stand, be valid
timor, timoris *m.*: fear, dread
triticum, -i *n.*: wheat
vas, vasis *n.*: a vessel
vexo (1): to harass

---

presente lupo: abl. abs., "the wolf being present"
sic jubet esse lupus: "the wolf orders things to be thus" i.e. he agrees
jubenti: dat. in i.o. after paret, "obeys *the one ordering* such things"
die fixo: abl. of time when, "on a fixed day"
metu: abl. of manner with facta, "made *with fear*"

Me decuit, presente lupo, quaecumque fateri;
　　Me decuit fraudem pellere fraude pari."
Cum timor in promptu sedeat, promissa timoris
　　Arent: nil fidei verba timentis habent.

areo (2): to wither
decet (2) decuit: it is fitting, right
fateor (2): to admit, confess
fraus, fraudis f.: fraud
habeo (2): to have, hold
par, paris (gen.): equal

pello (3): to beat, drive out
promissum, -i n.: promise
promptus, -us m.: visibity, readiness
sedeo (2): to sit
timeo (2): to fear
verbum, -i n.: a word

fateri: pres. inf. dep. after decuit, "it was fitting *to say* whatever"
fraude pari: abl.of means, "drive out *with an equal fraud*"
cum sedeat: pres. subj. in cum circumstantial, "when fear remains"
in promptu: "in visibility" i.e. is present
fidei: gen. partitive, "have nothing *of faith*"

Fable 32: De calvo et musca

A fly buzzes around the head of a bald man, who strikes himself in an effort to hit the fly. The fly laughs at the man, and it appears that once again the animal is the smarter character, until the man points out that he can strike himself many times without harm, while one hit will kill the fly. The moral reminds that a great injury (death to the fly) can come from a little injury (the fly annoying the man).

Musca premit calvum; muscam vult cedere calvus.

Ut muscam feriat, se ferit; illa redit.

Calvus ait: "Te Parca jubet vicina jocari.

Si ferior rides, si feriare cades;

Sospes ero decies ictus, semel icta peribis.

Est mea prompta mihi gratia, surda tibi."

Jure potest laedi laedens ut laedat: in illum,

Unde brevis coepit laesio, magna redit.

---

brevis, breve: little, small
cado (3): to fall, die
calvus, -i *m.*: a bald person
cedo (3): to go away
coepio (3): to begin, starts
decem: 10 times
ferio (4): to hit, strike
gratia, -ae *f.*: favor
ico (3) **ici, ictus**: hit, strike
jocor (1): to pester
jus, juris *n.*: law, legal system
laedo (3): to strike, hurt
laesio, laesionis *f.*: injury, harm
magnus, -a -um: large, great

musca, -ae *f.*: a fly
Parca, -ae *f.*: Fate
pereo (4): to die
premo (3): to press
promptus, -a, -um: manifest, evident
redeo (4): to return
rideo (2): to laugh at
semel: one time . once
sospes, -pitis (*gen.*): safe and sound
surdus, -a, -um: falling on deaf ears, stupid
unde: from where
vicinus, -a, -um: neighboring
volo, velle: wish (+ *inf.*)

---

ut feriat: pres. subj. in purpose clause, "in order to strike"
Parca vicina: "neighboring or related fate" i.e. as explained in the next lines
si feriare: pres. subj. in future more vivid protasis, "if you were to be struck"
ictus ... icta: perf. part. conditional, "if you ... if I *having been hit*"
laedi: pres. pass. inf. after *potest*, "is able *to be hurt*"
laedens: pres. part., nom. subject, "the one striking"
ut laedat: pres. subj. in purpose clause, "striking *in order to hurt*"
unde: (= *ex quo*), "against that one *from which*"

Fable 33: De vulpe et ciconia

Rather than portraying one character as a villain and one as a hero, this fable portrays a matching of wits. A fox invites a stork over for a meal, but only serves liquid food, so the stork is unable to eat it. The stork in turn invites the fox over, but serves food at the bottom of a glass jar, so that the fox is unable to reach the food. The moral, of course, repeats the familiar "do unto others" idiom.

> Vulpe vocante, venit speratque ciconia cenam;
>
> > Fallit avem liquidus, vulpe jocante, cibus.
>
> Cum bibat ista cibos, solum bibit illa dolorem:
>
> > Hic dolor in vulpem fabricat arma doli.
>
> Sunt pauci mora pauca dies; avis inquit: "Habemus
>
> > Fercula quae sapiunt: dulcis amica, veni."
>
> Haec venit; haec vase vitreo bona fercula condit,
>
> > At solam recipit formula vasis avem.

---

amica, -ae *f.*: a friend
arma, -orum *n.*: arms, weapons
avis, avis *f.*: a bird
bibo (3): to drink
cena, -ae *f.*: dinner
cibus, -i *m.*: food
ciconia, -ae *f.*: a stork
condo (3): to contain
dolor, doloris *m.*: pain
dolus, -i *m.*: a trick
dulcis, dulce: sweet
fabrico (1): to build
fallo (3): to deceive
ferculum, -i *n.*: food

formula, -ae *f.*: a shape
joco (1): to joke
liquidus, -a, -um: liquid, flowing
paucus, -a -um: little
recipio (3): to keep back
sapio (3): to taste of, be tasty
solus, -a, -um: only
spero (1): to hope for
vas, vasis *n.*: a vessel, dish
venio (4): to come
vitreus, -a, -um: of glass
voco (1): to call
vulpes, vulpis *f.*: a fox

---

vulpe vocante: abl. abs., "the fox calling"
vulpe jocante: abl. abs., "the fox playing joke"
cum bibat: pres. subj. in cum circumstantial, "when that one drinks that food"
bibit dolorem: "he drinks grief" i.e. because he is unable to drink with his long beak"
dolor ... doli: an example of *figura etymologica*
mora pauca: nom. pred., "are a *small delay*"
vase vitreo: abl. of place where, "in a dish of glass"
formula: nom., "*the shape* of the dish" i.e. with a long narrow neck

Laudat opes oculo vasis nitor; has negat ori

 Formula: sic geminat visus odorque famem.

Sic vulpes jejuna redit, sic fallitur audens

 Fallere, sic telo laeditur ipsa suo.

Quod tibi non faceres alii fecisse caveto,

 Vulnera ne facias quae potes ipse pati.

audeo (2): to intend, dare to (+ *inf.*)
caveo (2): to beware not to (+ *inf.*)
facio (3) **feci**: do, cause
fames, famis *f.*: hunger
gemino (1): to double, repeat
jejunus, -a -um: hungry
laudo (1): to recommend (+ *dat.*)
nego (1): to deny, refuse (+ *dat.*)
nitor, nitoris *m.*: brightness, splendor

oculus, -i *m.*: an eye
odor, -is *m.*: a scent, odor
ops, opis *f.*: resources, wealth
os, oris *n.*: a mouth
patior, (3): suffer
telum, -i *n.*: a weapon
visus, visus *m.*: appearance
vulnus, vulneris *n.*: a wound

laudat ... nitor: "the splendor praises" i.e. it recommends to the eye

visus odorque: "*the sight and odor* (each) doouble"

jejuna: nom. pred., "the wolf returns *hungry*"

telo suo: abl. of means, "is wounded *by her own weapon*" i.e. by her own joke

quod faceres: imperf. subj. in relative clause of characteristic, "*what you would not do to yourself*"

fecisse: perf. inf. after *caveto*, "beware *to have done* to another"

caveto: 3rd person imper., "let him beware"

ne facias: pres. subj. in prohibition, "*don't cause* wounds"

Fable 34: De lupo et capite

In this strange fable a wolf happens upon a bust, which he believes to be a human head. The wolf laments that the head is without a voice and without a mind. The moral has a rather religious tone, stating that the only brightness in the world is the soul, ignoring any potential moral about the ignorance of the wolf.

Dum legit arva lupus, reperit caput arte superbum;

Hoc beat humanis ars pretiosa genis.

Hoc lupus alterno volvit pede, verba resolvit:

"O sine voce genas, o sine mente caput!

Fuscat et extinguit cordis caligo nitorem

Corporis: est animi solus in orbe nitor.

---

alternus, -a, -um: one of two
animus, -i *m.*: mind
ars, artis *f.*: skill, art
arvum, -i *n.*: a field
beo (1): to bless, enrich
caligo, caliginis *f.*: mist, darkness
caput, capitis *n.*: a head, bust of a head
cor, cordis *n.*: a heart
corpus, corporis *n.*: a body, person
extinguo (3): to extinguish
fusco (1): to darken
gena, -ae *f.*: cheeks
humanus, -a -um: human

lego (3): to pick over
lupus, -i *m.*: a wolf
mens, mentis *f.*: mind
nitor, -oris *m.*: splendor
orbis, orbis *m.*: world
pes, pedis *m.*: a foot
pretiosus, -a, -um: expensive, costly
reperio (4): to discover, learn
resolvo (3): to loosen, release
superbus, -a, -um: arrogant, haughty
volvo (3): roll
vox, vocis *f.*: voice, tone, expression

---

arte: abl. of specification, "superb *in its art*" i.e. artfully made"
humanis genis: abl. of means, "enriches *with human cheeks*"
alterno pede: abl. of means, "with alternate foot" i.e. now this way, now that
animi: gen. pred., "is *of the mind*"

Fable 35: De graculo et pavone

The animal interactions in this fable are rather predictable; a grackle dresses as the more beautiful peacock until he is eventually caught and stripped. The moral, however, must have been of great importance to the medieval readers, as the last eight lines of the fable are marked with paragraph symbols in a number of the manuscripts. The moral warns against attempts to rise beyond your own station, for such is sure to lead to a great fall. This moral seems to have heavy Biblical overtones, and would certainly resonate with medieval audiences.

Graculus, invento picti pavonis amictu,

    Se polit et socias ferre superbit aves.

Quem fore pavonem pavonis penna fatetur,

    Pavonum generi non timet ire comes.

Pavo dolum sentit, falsi pavonis honorem

    Increpat et domitam verbere nudat avem.

Nuda latet sociosque fugit minuique pudorem

---

amictus, amictus *m.*: a cloak, clothing
comes, comitis *m./f.*: comrade, companion
dolus, -i *m.*: a trick
domo (1): to subdue
eo, ire: to go
falsus, -a, -um: wrong, false
fateor (2): to admit, confess
fero, ferre: to bear, suffer
fugio (3): to flee, run away (+ *inf.*)
genus, generis *n.*: kind, race
graculus, -i *m.*: a jackdaw
honor, honoris *m.*: honor
increpo (1): to rebuke
invenio (4) **veni, ventus**: to discover
lateo (2): to lie hidden

minuo (3): to lessen, reduce
nudo (1): to lay bare, strip
nudus, -a, -um: naked
pavo, pavonis *m.*: a peacock
penna, -ae *f.*: a feather, wing
pictus, -a, -um: painted, colored
polio (4): to smooth, polish
pudor, pudoris *m.*: decency, shame
sentio (4): to perceive
socia, -ae *f.*: a companion
socius, -i *m.*: an associate, companion
superbio (4): to disdain to (+ *inf.*)
timeo (2): to fear (+ *inf.*)
verber, verberis *n.*: a blow

---

invento amictu: abl. abs., "the clothing having been discovered"
se polit: "decorated himself"
fore: fut. inf. after *fatetur*, "whom the feather claimed *to be*"

Sic putat; hanc duro corripit ore comes:

"Ascensor nimius nimium ruit, aptus in imis

Est locus: haec levis est, illa ruina gravis.

Qui plus posse putat sua quam natura ministrat,

Posse suum superans, se minus esse potest.

Si tibi nota satis naturae meta fuisset,

Non vilis nec inops nec sine veste fores."

Cui sua non sapiunt, alieni sedulus auceps

Quod non est rapiens, desinit esse quod est.

---

alienus, -i *m.*: other, another
aptus, -a, -um: suitable
ascensor, ascensoris *m.*: one who ascends
auceps, -ipis *m.*: a bird-catcher, grasper
corripio (3): to seize, grasp
desino (3): to cease, desist (+ *inf.*)
durus, -a -um: harsh
gravis, grave: heavy, painful
imus, -a, -um: lowest
inops, inopis (*gen.*): weak, poor
levis, leve: light, smooth
locus, -i *m.*: seat, rank
meta, -ae *f.*: a boundary
ministro (1): to provide

minus, minor: less than (+ *abl.*)
natura, -ae *f.*: nature
nimius, -a, -um: excessive, too great
notus, -a, -um: known
os, oris *n.*: a mouth
rapio (3): to drag off, snatch
ruina, -ae *f.*: a fall
ruo (3): to destroy, ruin
sapio (3): to be tasty
satis: enough
sedulus, -a, -um: persistent, greedy
supero (1): to overcome
vestis, vestis *f.*: clothing
vilis, -e: cheap, common

comes: nom. pred., "to go *as a companion*"
verbere: abl. of means, "subdued *with a blow*"
minui: pres. pass. inf. after *putat*, "she thinks her decency *to be diminished*"
duro ore: abl. of manner, "grasps *with a harsh mouth*"
haec...illa: "the latter...the former" i.e. the ascent ... the ruin
plus...quam: "more...than"
sua natura: nom. subj. of *ministrat*, "than *his own nature* provides"
posse suum: inf. as noun, "exceeding *his own ability*"
minus: nom. pred., "to be *less than* himself"
si ... fuisset: plupf. subj. past contrafactual protasis, "if the boundary *had been known*"
fores: impf. subj. in present contrafactual apodosis, "you would not be"
cui sua non sapiunt: "the one *to whom his own things are not tasty*"
alieni auceps: "the grasper of another" but also, "the bird-catcher of another (bird)"
rapiens: pres. part. instrumental, "*by snatching* what he is not"

Fable 36: De mula et musca

As is often the case, this fable has the same basic lesson as the preceding fable. Here, it is a fly that tries to rise above his station, giving orders to the mule. The mule responds that he only takes direction from his master, and the fly is put back into his humble position. The moral, however takes a slightly different approach, stating that weak men often assert themselves against the strong, but rarely are effective.

Mula rapit cursum: nam mulam mulio cogit.

Mulae musca nocet vulnere sive minis:

"Cur pede sopito cursum tempusque moraris?

Te premo, te pungo: pessima, curre levis.

Mula refert: "Quia magna tonas? Vis magna videri?

Nec tua facta nocent, nec tua verba mihi,

Nec te sustineo, sed eum, quem sustinet axis,

---

axis, axis *m.*: an axis, chariot
cogo (3): to force, compel
cur: why?
curro (3): to run
cursus, cursus *m.*: a running, way
factum, -i *n.*: a fact, deed
levis, -e: smooth, light
magnus, -a, -um: great
mina, -ae *f.*: threats
moror (1): to delay
mula, -ae *f.*: a mule
mulio, mulionis *m.*: a muleteer, mule driver
musca, -ae *f.*: a fly

noceo (2): to harm, hurt (+ *dat.*)
pes, pedis *m.*: a foot
pessimus, -a, -um: worst
premo (3): to press
pungo (3): prick, sting
refero, referre: return
sopitus, -a, -um: sleepy
sustineo (2): to put up with, support
tempus, temporis *n.*: time
tono (1): to thunder
verbum, -i *n.*: a word
videor (2): to seem

---

rapit cursum: "he hurries on his way"
mulam mulio: *figura etymologica*
pede sopito: abl. of manner, "with a sleepy foot"
mulae: dat. after nocent, "harms *the mule*"
levis: nom. with adverbial force, "he runs *lightly*"
vis: pres. of *volo*, "do you wish" +inf.
nec tua ... nec tua/ qui mea ... qui mea: examples of *anadiplosis*, "doubling"

Qui mea frena tenet, qui mea terga ferit.

Audet in audacem timidus fortique minatur

Debilis, audendi dum videt esse locum.

audax, audacis (*gen.*): bold
debilis, debile: weak
ferio (4): to hit
fortis, forte: strong
frenum, -i *n.*: a bridle

locus, -i *m.*: a place
minor (1): to threaten
teneo (2): to hold
tergum, -i *n.*: a back
timidus, -a, -um: timid, fearful

audet in audacem: "he dares against a daring one" a *figura etymologica*
forti: dat. after *minatur*, "threatens *the strong*"
audendi: gerund gen. with *locum*, "an opportunit *of daring*"

80

Fable 37: De musca et formica

This fable is as close as the elegiac Romulus comes to the now-popular fable of the ant and the grasshopper. Here it is a fly rather than a grasshopper that is inciting the ant; the fly seeks to glorify her own lifestyle by talking about the glories of flying, and the royal tables that she is able to take food from. The ant retaliates by noting that although her lifestyle may be more humble, she always has a guaranteed next meal, and she is not forced to live as a thief. The moral, however, does not glorify the humble lifestyle of the ant as might be expected. Instead, it warns to watch the tongue, for sweet words produce sweetness, while words spoken in hatred continue to produce hate.

Musca movens lites formicam voce fatigat,

Se titulis ornat turpiter ipsa suis:

Torpes mersa cavis, levitas mihi queritur alis;

Dat tibi fossa domum, nobilis aula mihi.

Deliciae sunt grana tuae, me regia nutrit

Mensa; bibis fecem, sed bibo lene merum.

---

ala, -ae *f.*: a wing
aula, -ae *f.*: a hall
bibo (3): to drink
cavum, -i *m.*: a cave, hole
deliciae, -arum *f.*: pleasure, delight
domus, -i *f.*: a house
faex, faecis *f.*: dregs, grounds
fatigo (1): to weary
formica, -ae *f.*: an ant
fossa, -ae *f.*: a ditch
granum, -i *n.*: a grain, seed
lenis, -e: smooth, mild
levitas, levitatis *f.*: lightness
lis, litis *n.*: a quarrel

mensa, -ae *f.*: a table
mergo (3) mersi, mersus: to immerse
merum, -i *n.*: wine (unmixed with water)
moveo (2): to move
musca, -ae *f.*: a fly
nobilis, nobile: noble
nutrio (4): to nourish, feed
orno (1): to equip, decorate
quaero (3): to seek
regius, -a, -um: royal
titulus, -i *m.*: title, honor
torpeo (2):, be struck motionless from fear
turpiter: shamelessly
vox, vocis *f.*: a voice

---

voce: abl. of means, "wearies *with his voice*"
se ... ipsa suis: *she herself* decorates *herself with her own* titles"
mersa: perf. part. nom., "you *immersed* in caves"
alis: abl. of means, "is sought *with my wings*"
grana: nom. pred., "your delights are *seeds*"

Quod bibis a limo sugis; mihi suggerit aurum

    Quod bibo. Saxa premis, regia serta premo.

Sede, cibis, potu, thalamis cum regibus utor,

    Reginae teneris oscula figo genis."

Non minus urentes mittit formica sagittas

    Et sua non modicum spicula fellis habent:

"Ludo mersa cavis: nescit tua penna quietem.

    Sunt mihi pauca satis: sunt tibi multa parum.

Me laetam videt esse cavus: te regia tristem.

    Plus mihi grana placent quam tibi regis opes.

Venatur mihi farra labor: tibi fercula furtum.

---

aurum, auri *n.*: gold	**penna, -ae** *f.*: a feather, wing
cibus, -i *m.*: food	**placeo** (2): to please
far, farris *n.*: grain	**plus ... quam**: more ... than
fel, fellis *n.*: poison	**potus, potus** *m.*: a drink
ferculum, -i *n.*: food	**premo** (3): to press, pursue
figo (3): to fix	**quies, quietis** *f.*: quiet
formica, -ae *f.*: an ant	**regia, -ae** *f.*: a palace
furtum, -i *n.*: theft	**regina, -ae** *f.*: a queen
gena, -ae *f.*: cheeks	**rex, regis** *m.*: a king
habeo (2): to have	**sagitta, -ae** *f.*: an arrow
labor, laboris *m.*: labor	**saxum, -i** *n.*: a stone
laetus, -a, -um: happy	**sedes, sedis** *f.*: a seat, home
limus, -i *m.*: mud, mire	**sertum, serti** *n.*: a wreath
ludo (3): to play	**spiculum, -i** *n.*: a sting
minor, -us: smaller	**suggero** (3): to carry, furnish
mitto (3): to send, throw	**sugo** (3): to suck
modicus, -i *m.*: a small amount	**tener, -a, -um**: tender, delicate
nescio (4): to not know	**thalamus, -i** *m.*: a bedroom
ops, opis *f.*: wealth	**tristis, triste**: sad, sorrowful
osculum, -i *n.*: a kiss	**uro** (3): to burn
parum: too little	**utor** (3): to use, enjoy (+ *abl.*)
paucus, -a -um: little	**venor** (1) **venatus sum**: hunt, seek after

---

premis ... saxa: "you press on rocks" i.e. when you sleep

teneris genis: abl. of place where, "fix kisses *on the tender cheek*"

sunt mihi ... sunt tibi: note *antithesis* in each line

laetam...tristem: acc. pred., "sees me to be *happy*... you to be *sad*" i.e. I am happy in the cave, you are sad in the palace

plus...quam: "seeds please *more...than* wealth"

Haec mihi pax mellit: toxicat illa timor.

Mundo farre fruor: tu foedas omnia tactu.

Cum nulli noceam, cuilibet una noces.

Est mea parcendi speculum: tua vita vorandi.

Sunt mea quae carpo: non nisi rapta voras.

Ut comedas vivis: comedo ne vivere cessem.

Me nihil infestat: te fugat omnis homo.

Unde petis vitam, rapitur tibi vita; palato

Dulcia vina bibens, fel necis acre bibis.

---

acer, **acris**: sharp, bitter
carpo (3): to seize
cesso (1): to cease from (+ *inf.*)
comedo (3): to eat, consume
cuilibet: whomever (*dat.*)
dulcis, dulce: sweet
far, farris *n.*: husked wheat
fel, fellis *n.*: poison
foedo (1): to defile
fruor (3): to enjoy (+ *abl.*)
fugo (1): to chase away, flee
homo, hominis *m.*: a man
infesto (1): to harass
mello (3): to sweeten
mundus, -a, -um: clean
nex, necis *f.*: death

nihil: nothing
nullus, nulli *m.*: no one
palatum, -i *n.*: palate, sense of taste
parco (3): to forbear, show
pax, pacis *f.*: peace, harmony
peto (3): to attack
speculum, -i *n.*: a mirror
tactus, tactus *m.*: touch
timor, timoris *m.*: fear, dread
toxico (1): to posion
unde: from where
unus, -a -um: alone
vinum, -i *n.*: wine
vita, -ae *f.*: life
vivo (3): to live, survive
voro (1): to swallow, devour

---

farre: abl. after *fruor*, "I enjoy my *husk*"
tactu: abl. of means, "with your touch"
cum...noceam: pres. subj. in *cum* circumstantial, "while I harm no one"
parcendi ... vorandi: gerunds gen., "mirror *of sparing* ... life *of devouring*"
non nisi: litotes, "you do *not* eat *unless*" i.e. you only eat
comedas ... cessem: pres. subj. in purpose clauses, "in order to eat ... lest I cease"
palato: dat. of specification, "sweet *to the palate*"
bibens: pres. part. instrumental, "*by drinking* you drink"

Si negat ala tibi ventoso victa flabello,

    Aut nece vinciris, aut semiviva jaces.

Si potes aestivi dono durare favoris,

    Cetera si parcant, non tibi parcit hiems.

Dulcia pro dulci, pro turpi turpia reddi

    Verba solent: odium lingua fidemque parit.

aestivus, -a, -um: summery, summer
ala, alae *f.*: a wing
ceterus, -a, -um: the other
donum, -i *n.*: a gift, present
dulcis, -e: sweet
duro (1): to harden
favor, favoris *m.*: favor
fides, fidei *f.*: faith, loyalty
flabellum, -i *n.*: a small fan
hiems, hiemis *f.*: winter, winter time
jaceo (2): to lie, lie down

lingua, -ae *f.*: a tongue, speech
nego (1): to deny, fail (+ *dat.*)
odium, -i *n.*: hate, hatred
parco (3): to spare
pario (3): bear, give birth to
reddo (3): to return, restore
semivivus, -a, -um: half-alive, almost dead
soleo (2): to be in the habit of (+ *inf.*)
turpis, -e: ugly, nasty
ventosus, a, um: windy
vinco (3): to conquer, defeat

ventoso flabello: abl. of means, "conquered *with the windy fan*"
aestivi favoris: "gift of summery kindness" transferred epithet
parcant: pres. subj. in present general conditional, "if others are sparing"
reddi: pres. inf. pass. complementing solent, "are in the habit of *being returned*"

Fable 38: De lupo et vulpe

Here, the two greatest villains of the fable collection meet, but it is only the wolf that is wicked in this fable. The fox is accused of theft, but is acquitted by the judge, an ape, by his virtuous living. The moral condemns living without a sense of truth, which is apparently what has motivated the wolf's accusation. The implication is that the filthy lifestyle of the wolf has proven him to be an unsavory character repeatedly, and so the judge is unable to take his claim seriously.

> Respondere lupo de furti labe tenetur
>
> Vulpes; causa vocat: hic petit, ille negat.
>
> Simius est judex; docti non errat acumen
>
> Judicis: arcanum mentis in ore legit.
>
> Judicium figit: "Poscis quod poscere fraus est
>
> Visque fidem de re quam negat ipsa fides.
>
> Tu bene furta negas: te vitae purior usus

---

acumen, acuminis *n.*: sharpened point, fraud
arcanum, -i *n.*: a secret
causa, -ae *f.*: a cause, motive
doctus, -a -um: learned, cunning, shrewd
erro (1): to wander, go astray
fides, -i *f.*: faith
figo (3): to establish
fraus, fraudis *f.*: fraud
furtum, -i *n.*: theft
judex, judicis *m.*: a judge
judicium, -i *n.*: a judgment, sentence
labes, labis *f.*: disaster, debacle
lego (3): to read, gather

lupus, -i *m.*: a wolf
mens, mentis *f.*: mind
os, oris *n.*: a mouth, expression
peto (3): to attack
posco (3): to ask, demand
purus, -a, -um: pure, clean
respondeo (2): to answer
simius, -i *m./f.*: ape
usus, usus *m.*: use, enjoyment
vita, -ae: life
voco (1): to call
vulpes, vulpis *f.*: a fox

---

lupo: dat. after *respondere,* "respond *to the wolf*"
poscere: inf. epexegetic after *fraus,* "is a fraud *to demand*"
poscis: "you (the wolf) demand"
vis: 2 s. of *volo,* "you (the fox) wish" + inf.

Liberat. Hanc litem pax domet, ira cadat."
Simplicitas veri fraus estque puerpera falsi:
Esse solent vitae disssona verba suae.
Sordibus imbuti nequeunt dimittere sordes.
Fallere qui didicit, fallere semper amat.

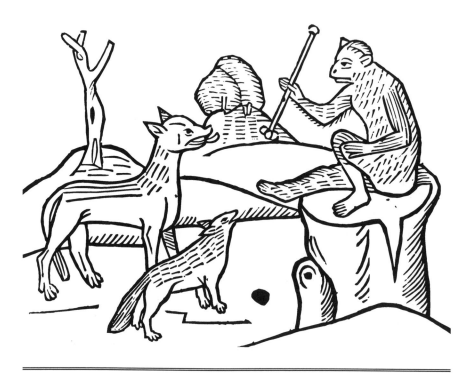

amo (1): to love (+ *inf.*)
cado (3): to decay, subside
dimitto (3): to dismiss, part with
disco (3) **didici**: learn, hear (+ *inf.*)
dissonus, -a, -um: discordant, different
domo (1): to subdue, master
fallo (3): to deceive
falsum, -i *n.*: falsehood
imbuo (3) **imbui, imbutus**: wet, soak
ira, -ae *f.*: anger
libero (1): to free, release

lis, litis *f.*: lawsuit, quarrel
nequeo (4): to be unable (+ *inf.*)
pax, pacis *f.*: peace, harmony
puerpera, -ae *f.*: a mother
semper: always
simplicitas, -tatis *f.*: innocence
soleo (2): to be accustomed (+ *inf.*)
sordes, sordis *f.*: filth, dirt
verum, -i *n.*: truth
vita, -ae *f.*: anger

domet ... cadat: pres. subj. jussive clause, "let peace *subdue* ... *let* anger *subside*"
simplicitas veri: "innocence of the truth" i.e. being unaware of the truth, a paradoxical metaphor
dissona: pred. nom., "are accustomed to be *discordant to*" + dat.

Fable 39: De rustico et mustela

The moral of the "Man and the Weasel" relies on rather complex logic, and again asks the reader to look into the soul of a man, just as in the earlier tale about the wolf and the bust. A weasel has been living in a man's house for a number of years, and as a result, the house has remained free of mice and other nuisances. The weasel cites this as a reason that the man might grant him particular favor. The man refuses however, noting that the deeds that the weasel has done may have been beneficial to him, but the animal did not do them with this in mind. He argues that in keeping the house clear of varmints, the weasel was only thinking of himself, as the mice filled his stomach. Furthermore, the man notes, the weasel allowed the mice to get plump on the man's bread before eating them, again thinking of his own stomach. The moral then notes that the fruit of a deed should not be counted as good unless the accompanying motives were good as well.

> Praeda viri, praedo murum mustela precatur:
>
> "Da veniam, debes parcere, parce mihi.
>
> Quod caret hoste domus, quod abest a sorde, fatetur
>
> Esse meum, pro me te rogat, ergo fave.

---

absum: to be away
careo (2): to lack, be without (+ *abl.*)
debeo (2): to owe
fateor (2): to admit, bear witness to (+ *inf.*)
faveo (2): to favor
hostis, -is *m/f.*: enemy
murus, -i *m.*: a wall, city wall
mustela, -ae *f.*: a weasel
parco: (3): to forbear, refrain from

praeda, -ae *f.*: prey, captured animal
praedo, praedonis *m.*: a robber, thief
precor (1): to beg
rogo (1): to ask, ask for
rusticus, -i *m.*: a peasant, farmer
sordes, sordis *f.*: filth, dirt
venia, -ae *f.*: favor, kindness
vir, viri *m.*: a man

---

praeda, praedo: nom. in apposition to *mustella*, the subj. of *precatur*, "a captured animal, a thief, a weasel" Note the *figura etymologica*

da ... mihi: the three pairs of words in this verse all mean the same thing, an example of *pleonasm*

hoste: abl. of separation after *caret*: "the house lacks *an enemy*"

meum (sc. donum): "bears witness that it is *my* (gift)"

rogat: pres., "(your home) *asks* you"

Servitio me redde tuo, mihi redde laboris

    Praemia, pro dono sit mea vita mihi."

"Ille refert: "Operum debetur gratia menti,

    Non operi: gratum mens bona reddit opus.

Nemo, licet prosit, nisi vult prodesse, meretur:

    Nam prodesse potest hostis, obesse putans.

Cum mihi prodesses, mihi non prodesse volebas:

    Hostibus ipsa meis et meis hostis eras;

Non mihi, monstra necans, sed eras tibi provida soli;

    Sic panem poteras rodere sola meum.

---

debeo (2): to owe
donum, -i *n.*: a gift, present
gratia, -ae *f.*: gratitude, thanks
gratus, -a, -um: pleasing, acceptable
labos, laboris *m.*: labor
licet (2): it is permitted, one may
mens, mentis *f.*: mind, intention
mereo (2): to be deserving
monstrum, -i *n.*: a beast
neco (1): to kill, murder
obsum, obesse: to hurt, be an enemy to (+ *dat.*)

opus, operis *n.*: need, work
panis, panis *m.*: bread, loaf
praemium, - *n.*: reward
prosum, prodesse: to be useful
providus, -a, -um: providing for (+ *dat.*)
puto (1): to think, believe
reddo (3): to return
refero, referre: bring, reply
rodo (3): to gnaw, peck
servitium, -i *n.*: slavery, servitude
solus, -a, -um: only, alone
volo, velle: to wish, want (+ *inf.*)

---

tuo servitio: dat. after *redde*, "return me *to your service*"
pro dono: "in return for my gift"
sit: pres. subj. jussive, "*let* my life *be*"
menti ... operi: dat. ind. obj., "is owed *to the mind* not *to the deed*"
prosit: pres. subj. concessive after *licet*, "although it is useful"
prodesses: impf. subj. concessive, "*although you were useful* to me"
hostibus ...meis: dat., "you were an enemy *to my enemies*"
necans: pres. part. instrumental, "*by killing* beasts"
soli: dat. after *provida*, "providing for yourself *alone*"
sola: nom., "you *alone* were able"

Pane meo pinguis, mihi da pinguedinis usum:

 Damnis penso necem; digna perire peri."

Nil honorat factum nisi facti sola voluntas:

 Non operis fructum, sed noto mentis opus.

---

damnum, -i *n.*: loss, damage

dignus, -a, -um: suitable (+ *inf.*)

factum, facti *n.*: a fact, deed

fructus, fructus *m.*: enjoyment, reward

nil: nothing

noto (3): to observe, record

panis, panis *m.*: bread

penso (1): to weigh, judge

pereo (4): to die, pass away

pinguedo, -inis *f.*: abundance

pinguis, pingue: fat, rich

voluntas, voluntatis *f.*: will, desire

---

pane meo: abl. of cause, "you are fat *from my bread*"

damnis: abl., "*for your crimes* I judge"

perire: inf. epexegetic after *digna*, "you, worthy *to die*"

Fable 40: De rana et bove

A frog is jealous of the large size of an ox, so she swells herself. Her son employs her to stop, noting that there is no way that the size of the frog, even inflated, could compare to the ox. The frog becomes increasingly upset by this, and swells so greatly that she bursts. The moral for this fable, as to be expected, cautions the lesser from comparing themselves to the greater.

Aequari vult rana bovi: tumet ergo. Tumenti

Natus ait: "Cessa; prae bove tota nihil."

Rana dolet meliusque tumet; premit ille tumentem:

"Vincere non poteris, victa crepare potes."

Tertius iratam vexat tumor; illa tumoris

Copia findit eam: viscera rupta patent.

Cum majore minor conferri desinat et se

Consulat et vires temperet ipse suas.

---

aequo (1): to make equal to (+ *dat.*)
bos, bovis *f.*: a cow
cesso (1): to be remiss
confero, -ferre: to bring together, compare
consulo (3): to consult, consider
copia, -ae *f.*: plenty, abundance of (+ *gen.*)
crepo (1): to rattle, crack
desino (3): to stop, cease to (+ *inf.*)
doleo (2): to hurt, suffer pain
findo (3): to split, divide
iratus, -a -um: enraged, angered
major, -us: large, great
melior, -ius: better
minor, -us: smaller
natus, -i, m. son

nihil: nothing
pateo (2): to stand open, be open
premo (3): to press, press hard
rana, -ae *f.*: a frog
rumpo (3), **rumpsi, ruptus**: to burst, destroy
tempero (1): to moderate, control oneself
tertius -a -um: three
totus, -a, -um: whole, all
tumeo (2): to swell, be swollen with conceit
tumor, tumoris *m.*: a swelling
vexo (1): to shake, vex
vinco (3), **vixi, victus**: to conquer, outlast
vis, viris *f.*: strength
viscus, visceris *n.*: entrails

---

aequari: pres. inf. pass. after *vult*, "he wishes to be made equal to" + dat.
tumenti: pres. part. dat. ind. obj., "speaks *to the one swelling*"
prae bove: "before the cow," i.e. in comparison to a cow
conferri: pres. inf. pass. after *desinat*, "cease *to be compared*"
desinat: pres. subj. in jussive, "*let* the smaller *cease*" + inf.
consulat ... temperet: pres. subj. jussive, "let him consider ... let him moderate!"

Fable 41: De pastore et leone

This fable was taken from an ancient story found in the 2nd century *Attic Nights* of Aulus Gellius. In the tale, a man named Androcles helps an injured lion by removing a thorn from his foot. He is later repaid for his kindness when he is thrown into a pit of lions in punishment for fleeing slavery; the lion in the pit is, of course, the lion that he had helped earlier, who remembers Androcles' kind deed. The lion immediately behaves as though he is tame, and the astonished Romans free both the lion and Androcles. The fable version of this story is told almost exactly as the ancient tale, except that Androcles is recast as an unnamed shepherd, and the crime that sends him to the lion's den is unnamed. The moral repeats the adage of doing unto others. This story retains popularity in the Middle Ages outside of the elegiac Romulus, and versions of it can be found in Chretien de Troyes' romances, as well as in the *Gesta Romanorum*. The story remained so popular that George Bernard Shaw turned the narrative into a play in 1912 (*Ashliman, Androcles and the Lion*).

Sollicitus praedae currit leo; spina leonem

Vulnerat; offendit, in pede mersa, pedem.

Fit mora de cursu: levitas improvida lapsum

Saepe facit; laeso stat pede turba pedum.

---

curro (3): to run, hurry
cursus, cursus *m.*: running
fio, fieri: to happen, made
improvidus, -a, -um: thoughtless, unwary
laedo (3) **laesi, laesus**: strike, hurt
lapsus, lapsus *m.*: a slip, fall
leo, leonis *m.*: a lion
levitas, levitatis *f.*: levity, lightness
mergo (3) **mersi, mersus**: dip, plunge
mora, -ae *f.*: delay, hindrance

offendo (3): to offend
pastor, pastoris *m.*: a shepherd, herdsman
pes, pedis *m.*: a foot
praeda, -ae *f.*: booty, prey
sollicitus, -a, -um: concerned, worried
spina, -ae *f.*: a thorn
sto (1): to stand
turba, turbae *f.*: a crowd
vulnero (1): to wound

---

praedae: dat. after *sollicitus*, "concerned *for prey*"
mersa: perf. part., "the thorn, *having been plunged in*"
laeso pede: abl. abs., "his foot having been hurt"
turba pedum: "the crowd of his feet" i.e. all four feet

91

Vix aegrum sinit ire dolor saniemque fatetur;

Major idem loquitur vulneris ipse dolor.

Cum laedit miseros, fortuna medetur eisdem:

Hoc est cur medicum plaga leonis habet.

Nam leo pastorem reperit, pastorque leoni

Pro dape tendit oves. Respuit ille dapes;

Supplicat et plagam tenso pede monstrat et illi

Orat opem; pastor vulnera solvit acu.

Exit cum sanie dolor et res causa doloris;

Hic blando medicam circuit ore manum,

Sospes abit meritique notas in corde sigillat.

---

abeo: depart, go away
acus, acus *f.*: a needle, pin
aeger, -gra, -grum: sick
blandus, -a -um: flattering, coaxing
causa, -ae *f.*: a cause, source
circueo, circuire: encircle, surround
cor, cordis *n.*: a heart, mind
cur: why?
dapis, -is *f.*: a feast
dolor, doloris *m.*: pain, anguish
exeo, exire: to leave, pass
fateor (2): to disclose, bear witness to
fortuna, -ae *f.*: chance, luck
loquor (3): to speak, tell
major, -us: larger, greater
manus, manus *f.*: a hand
medeor (2): to heal, cure
medicus, -a, -um: healing
medicus, -i *m.*: a healer
meritum, -i *n.*: merit

miser, -a, -um: poor, miserable
monstro (1): to show, point out
nota, -ae *f.*: a mark, sign
ops, opis *f.*: help
oro (1): to beg, ask for
os, oris *n.*: a mouth, speech
ovis, ovis *f.*: a sheep
plaga, -ae *f.*: a wound
reperio (4): to discover
respuo (3): to reject, spit
sanies, saniei *f.*: bloody matter, wound
sigillo (1): to seal, confirm
sino (3): to allow, permit (+ *inf.*)
solvo (3): to loosen, free
sospes, sospitis (*gen.*): safe and sound
supplico (1): to pray, supplicate
tendo (3): to stretch, offer to (+ *dat.*)
tendo (3) **tensi, tensus**: to stretch, spread
vix: hardly, barely
vulnus, vulneris *n.*: a wound

---

aegrum: acc. subject of *ire*, "allows *the sick one* to go"
eisdem: dat. after *medetur*, "cures *the same people*"
leoni: dat. of advantage, "for the lion"
tenso pede: abl. abs., "his foot having been stretched out"

Tempore deleri gratia firma nequit.

Hic leo vincla subit. Romanae gloria praedae

Hunc habet et multas miscet arena feras.

Ecce necis poenam pastori culpa propinat:

Clauditur in mediis et datur esca feris.

Hunc leo presentit, petit hunc. Timet ille; timenti

Haec fera blanditur; sperat, abitque timor.

Nil feritatis habens, ludit fera, cauda resultat.

Dum fera mansuescit, se negat esse feram.

Hunc tenet, hunc lingit pensatque salute salutem:

Nulla sinit fieri vulnera, nulla facit.

---

arena, -ae *f.*: sand, arena
blandior (4): to flatter (+ *dat.*)
cauda, -ae *f.*: a tail
claudo (3): to close, shut
culpa, -ae *f.*: a fault, crime
deleo (2): to erase, wipe
esca, -ae *f.*: food, meat
fera, -ae *f.*: a wild beast, animal
feritas, feritatis *f.*: wildness
fio, fieri: to happen, come about
firmus, -a -um: firm, steady
gloria, -ae *f.*: glory, fame
gratia, -ae *f.*: favor, goodwill
lingo (3): to lick, lick up
ludo (3): to play, tease, trick
mansuesco (3): to become tame
medius, -a, -um: middle, center
misceo (2): to mix, mingle
multus, -a -um, large, intense
nego (1): to deny, refuse
nequeo (4): be unable

nex, necis *f.*: death
nullus, -a, -um: no
penso (1): to compensate X (*acc.*) with Y (*abl.*)
peto (3): to seek, approach
poena, -ae *f.*: a penalty, punishment
praeda, -ae *f.*: booty, loot
praesentio (4): to recognize
propino (1): to pledge X (*acc.*) to Y (*dat.*)
resulto (1): to wag
Romanus, -a, -um: Roman
salus, salutis *f.*: health, prosperity
sino (3): to allow, permit (+ *inf.*)
spero (1): to hope
subeo (4): submit to
tempus, temporis *n.*: time
teneo (2): to hold, keep
timeo (2): to fear, dread
timor, timoris *m.*: fear, dread
vinclum, -i *n.*: a chain, bond

---

tempore: abl. of means, "by time"
deleri: inf. pass. after *nequit*, "is unable *to be erased*"
esca: pred. nom., "is given *as food*"
feris: either abl. (with *in mediis*), "in the middle *of the beasts*" or dat. after *datur*, "given *to the beasts*"
timenti: dat. after *blanditur*, "he flatters *the one fearing*"

Roma stupet parcitque viro parcitque leoni.

Hic redit in silvas et redit ille domum.

Non debet meritum turpis delere vetustas:

Accepti memores nos decet esse boni.

acceptum, -i *n.*: favor
bonus, -a -um: good, honest
decet (2): to it is fitting, right (+ *inf.*)
deleo (2): to erase, wipe
domus, -i *f.*: a house
memor, memoris: remembering, grateful (+ *gen.*)
meritum, meriti *n.*: merit, value

parco (3): to spare (+ *dat.*)
redeo (4): return, go back
Roma, -ae *f.*: Rome
silva, -ae *f.*: wood, forest
stupeo (2): to be astounded
turpis, -e: ugly, disgraceful
vetustas, vetustatis *f.*: old age
vir, viri *m.*: a man

Roma: "*Rome* sees" i.e. the Romans, an example of *metonymy*
se ... esse: ind. st., "denies *that he is a beast*"
domum: acc., "returns *home*"

94

Fable 42: De leone et equo

This fable also features a lion, but one notably less kind than in the previous fable. Here, the lion approaches a herd of horses, hoping to trick them into befriending him so that he might eat one. The horses, however, can sense the deceit and tell the lion that he has come at the perfect time, as one of them has stepped on a thorn and needs help from the lion to remove it. As soon as he bends to examine the hoof, the horse stomps on his head, rendering him senseless. When the lion regains his senses he acknowledges that he deserved this punishment, for he had feigned kindness to the horses with the intention of harming them. The moral emphasizes the importance of not pretending to be what one is not. The reoccurrence of the lion character, as well as the thorn stuck in a foot would not be lost on the medieval reader, a theme which is certainly repeated by the fabulist in order to emphasize the importance of intentions over deeds, a lesson which is set up in the earlier "Man and the Weasel."

> Tondet equus pratum, petit hunc leo. Causa leonem
>
> Haec movet, ut fiat esca leonis equus.
>
> Inquit equo: "Mi frater, ave, fruor arte medendi,
>
> Et comes et medicus sum tibi." Paret equus:
>
> Sentit enim fraudes et fraudi fraude resistit.
>
> Mente prius texens retia fraudis, ait:

---

ars, artis *f.*: skill, art
ave: hail!
comes, comitis *m./f.*: comrade, companion
equus, -i *m.*: a horse, steed
fio, fieri: to happen, be made
frater, fratris *m.*: a brother
fraus, fraudis *f.*: fraud, trickery
fruor (3): to enjoy, delight in (+ *abl.*)
inquit: he says
leo, leonis *m.*: a lion
medeor (2): to heal

medicus, -i *m.*: a doctor, physician
mens, mentis *f.*: mind, intellect
moveo (2): to move, agitate
pareo (2): to obey, yield to
peto (3): to attack
pratum, -i *n.*: a meadow
prior, prius: earlier
resisto (3): to pause, continue
sentio (4): to perceive, feel
texo (3): to weave
tondeo (2): to cut, clip, graze

---

ut fiat: pres. subj. in purp. clause, "in order for the horse to become food"
medendi: gerund gen., "art *of healing*"
fraudi: dat. after *resistit*, "he resists the fraud"
fraude: abl. of means, "by means of fraud" note the polyptoton

"Quaesitus placitusque venis, te temporis offert
  Gratia, te rogitat pes mihi sente gravis."
Hic favet, instat equo; subjecto vertice calcem
  Inprimit et sopit membra leonis equus.
Vix fugit ille sopor, vix audet vita reverti,
  Vix leo, colla movens, respicit. Hostis abest.
Se leo sic damnat: "Patior pro crimine poenam:
  Nam gessi speciem pacis et hostis eram."
Quod non es, non esse velis; quod es, esse fatere:
  Est male quod non est, qui negat esse quod est.

---

absum, abesse: to be away, absent
audeo (2): to dare to (+ *inf.*)
calx, calcis *m./f.*: heel
collum, -i *n.*: a neck, throat
crimen, criminis *n.*: crime, offense
damno (1): to pass judgment
fateor (2): to admit, confess
faveo (2): to favor, support
fugio (3): to flee, fly
gero (3) **gessi**: bear, carry
gravis, grave: heavy, painful
hostis, -is *m/f*: enemy
inprimo (3): to impress, imprint
insto (1): to be close to (+ *dat.*)
membrum, -i *n.*: a limb, organ
offero (3): to offer, present
patior (3): to suffer, allow
pax, pacis *f.*: peace, harmony
pes, pedis *m.*: a foot

placitus, -a, -um: pleasing
poena, -ae *f.*: penalty, punishment
quaero (3) **quaesivi, quaesitus**: search for, seek
respicio (3): to look back at, consider
rete, retis *n.*: a net, snare
revertor (3): to turn back, go back
rogito (1): to ask, inquire
sentis, sentis *m.*: a thorn, briar
sopio (4): to renders insensible by a blow
sopor, soporis *m.*: insensibility
species, -i *f.*: sight, appearance
subjicio (3) **-jeci, -jectus**: to throw under, bend down
venio (4): to come
vertex, verticis *m.*: crown (of his head)
vita, -ae *f.*: life
vix: hardly, scarcely
volo, velle: wish, want

---

temporis gratia: "*the favor of time* presents you" i.e. you come at a good time
sente: abl. of cause, "painful *from a thorn*"
equo: dat. after *instant*, "approaches *the horse*"
subiecto vertice: abl. abs., "the crown of his (the lion's) head having been bent down"
reverti: pres. inf. after *audet*, "dares *to return*"
velis: pres. subj. volative, "you ought not to wish" +inf.
fatere: 2 s. imper., "confess!" +inf.
est male: "*he is badly* what he is not" i.e. he plays the part badly
quod est: predicate clause after *esse*, "who denies to be *(that) which he is*" Note the mannered variations of forms of the verb *sum, esse* in these last two lines

Fable 43: De equo et asino

Now it is the character of the horse that is repeated for a number of fables; here, just as in the previous pairing, the horse turns from a wise, discerning character, to an overly proud animal. The horse in this fable is particularly proud of the nice bridle and saddle that his owner has given him, and brags about these trappings to an ass who carries a heavy load humbly. The ass ignores the threats, and as they both age, the glory of the horse declines. As he becomes less useful, his master replaces him, and he is stripped of his noble bridle and saddle, and is hooked to a work cart instead. The ass sees this, and asks the horse what has become of his noble appearance. The moral notes that it is best to learn to tolerate lesser things, for everything is fleeting, and he who is once rich can easily be made poor.

> Gaudet equus faleris, freno sellaque superbit;
>
> Ista quidem vestit aureus arma nitor.
>
> Obstat asellus equo; vicus premit artus asellum,
>
> Vexat onus, tardat natus eundo labor.
>
> Quod sibi claudit iter, sonipes inclamat asello:
>
> "Occurris domino, vilis aselle, tuo.

---

armum, -i *n.*: implements
artus, -a, -um: close, dense
asellus, -i *m.*: a donkey
asinus, -i *m.*: an ass, donkey
aureus, -a, -um: of gold
claudo (3): to closes in
dominus, -i *m.*: an owner, lord, master
falerae, falerarum *f.*: an ornament
frenus, -i *m.*: a bridle, harness
gaudeo (2): to be glad, rejoice (+ *abl.*)
inclamo (1): to cry out (+ *dat.*)
iter, itineris *n.*: a journey, path
nascor (3): to produce
nitor, nitoris *m.*: brightness, splendor

obsto (1): to oppose, comes before (+ *dat.*)
occurro: run to meet, oppose (+ *dat.*)
onus, oneris *n.*: a load
premo (3): to pursue, oppress
quidem: indeed
sella, -ae *f.*: a wagon seat, saddle
sonipes, sonipedis *m.*: a horse, steed
superbio (4): to be proud of (+ *abl.*)
tardo (1): to slows down
vestio (4): to clothe, decorate
vexo (1): to shake, jolt
vicus, -i *m.*: a street
vilis, -e: worthless

---

ista arma: acc. pl., "decorates *those implements*" i.e. the items mentioned in the previous line

eundo: gerund of *eo*, "produced *by going*"

asello: dat. ind. obj., "cries out *to the ass*"

97

Vix tibi do veniam de tanti crimine fastus;

    Cui via danda fuit libera, dignus eram."

Supplicat ille minis nutatque timore silendo

    Tutior et surda praeterit aure minas.

Summus equi declinat honor: dum vincere certat,

    Vincitur et cursum viscera rupta negant.

Privatur faleris, freno privatur honesto;

    Hunc premit assiduo raeda cruenta jugo,

Huic tergum macies acuit, labor ulcerat armos.

    Hunc videt inque jocos audet asellus iners:

---

acuo (3): to sharpen
armus, -i *m.*: a side, flank
assiduus, -a, -um: unremitting
auris, auris *f.*: an ear
certo (1): to contend, contest (+ *inf.*)
cruentus, -a, -um: bloody
cursus, cursus *m.*: running
declino (1): to diminishes
dignus, -a -um: worthy, deserving
falerae, falerarum *f.*: an ornament
fastus, fastus *m.*: destain, haughtiness
frenus: a bridle, harness
honestus, -a -um: distinguished, reputable
honor, honoris *m.*: honor, respect
iners, inertis (*gen.*): helpless, weak
jocus, -i *m.*: a joke, jest
jugum, -i *n.*: a yoke
liber, -a, -um: free, unconstrained
macies, maciei *f.*: leanness, poverty
mina, -ae *f.*: threats, menaces

nuto (1): to nod
praetereo, praeterire: pass by
privo (1): to deprive, rob, free
raeda, -ae: wagon
rumpo (3) **rupi, ruptus**: break, destroy
sileo (2): to be silent
summus, -a, -um: highest
supplico (1): to humbles oneself before (+ *dat.*)
surdus, -a, -um: deaf, muted
tantus, -a, -um: of such size, so great
tergum, -i *n.*: a back
timor, timoris *m.*: fear, dread
tutus, -a, -um: safe, prudent
ulcero (1): to cause to fester
venia, -ae *f.*: pardon
via, viae *f.*: a way, road, journey
video (2): to see, look at
vinco (3): to conquer
viscus, visceris *n.*: innards

---

fastus: gen. with *crimine*, "crime *of haughtiness*"
danda fuit: gerundive in passive periphrastic, "a free way *ought to have been given*"
timore: abl. of manner, "nods *with fear*"
silendo: gerund abl. of means, "safer *by being silent*"
surda aure: abl. of manner, "with a deaf ear"
faleris: abl. of separation, "he is deprived *of his ornaments*"
freno honesto: abl. of separation, "deprived *of his reputable harness*"
raeda cruenta: nom. subject, "*the bloody wagon* presses""

"Dic, sodes ubi sella nitens, ubi nobile frenum?

Cur est haec macies, cur fugit ille nitor?

Cur manet hic gemitus, cur illa superbia fugit?

Vindicat elatos justa ruina gradus:

Stare diu nec vis nec honor nec forma nec aetas

Sufficit in mundo. plus tamen ista placent.

Vive diu, sed vive miser, sociosque minores

Disce pati; risum det tua vita mihi."

Pennatis ne crede bonis; te nulla potestas

In miseros armet: nam miser esse potes.

---

aetas, aetatis *f.*: lifetime, age
armo (1): to rouse
bonum, -i *n.*: good
credo (3): to trust, entrust (+ *dat.*)
dico (3): to say
disco (3): to learn to (+ *inf.*)
diu: (for) a long time
elatos, -a, -um: lofty
forma, -ae *f.*: form
gemitus, gemitus *m.*: a groan, sigh
gradus, gradus *m.*: a step, position
justus, -a -um: just, fair
maneo (2): to remain, stay
minor, -us: smaller
miser, -a, -um: poor, miserable
mundus, -i *m.*: world
niteo (2): to shine

nobilis, nobile: noble
patior (3): to suffer, allow
pennatus, -a, -um: winged
placeo (2): to please, satisfy
potestas, potestatis *f.*: power, rule
risus, risus *m.*: laughter
ruina, -ae *f.*: fall, catastrophe
socius, -i *m.*: a companion, ally
sodes: if you do not mind, please
sufficio (3): to be sufficient, be able to (+ *inf.*)
superbia, -ae *f.*: arrogance, pride
vindico (1): to claim, vindicate
vis, viris *f.*: strength
vivus, -a, -um: alive

---

sodes: (= **si audes**): parenthetical, "if you please"
tergum acuit: sharpens his back (i.e. makes his bones protrude)
det: pres. subj. jussive, "*let your life give* laughter to me"
pennatis bonis: dat. after *crede*, "trust in *winged goods*" i.e. in fleeting goods
armet: pres. subj. jussive, "*let no power rouse* you against wretched people"

Fable 44: De quadrupedibus et avibus

Again, the horse appears in this fable, but this time only as a secondary character. The horses are engaged in a battle against the birds, and they appear poised to emerge victorious. A particular bird sees that he may be losing, and switches his allegiances to the horses. An eagle joins the birds, and adds to their strength, so that the birds are able to win the battle. The traitor is then revealed, and stripped of his feathers, and forced to fly only at night. The moral notes that no man can serve two masters. Although it is not explicitly noted, the description of the punishment the bird receives-- stripped of his feathers, and forced to fly only at night-- also fits the description for a bat. The medieval readers must have noted this, and this fable is often illustrated in later print versions with a woodcut of a bat.

Quadrupedes pugnant avibus, victoria nutat;

Spes onerata metu vexat utrumque gregem.

Linquit aves quae sumit avis de vespere nomen,

Nec timet oppositi castra juvare chori.

Armat aves aquilae virtus, et viribus implet

Et monitu; torpet altera turba metu.

---

alter, -a, -um: one (of two)
aquila, -ae *f.*: an eagle
avis, avis *f.*: a bird
castrum, -i *n.*: a camp, fort
chorus, -i *m.*: a group
grex, gregis *m./f.*: flock, herd
impleo (2): to fill up, satisfy
juvo (1): to help, assist
linquo (3): to leave, quit
metus, metus *m.*: fear, anxiety
monitus, monitus *m.*: a warning, command
nomen, nominis *n.*: a name
nuto (1): to waver, be in doubt

onero (1): to burden, oppress
oppono (3) **opposui, oppositus**: to oppose
pugno (1): to fight, dispute
quadrupes, quadrupedis *m./f.*: four-footed animals
spes, -i *f.*: hope
sumo (3): to take up, begin
timeo (2): to fear, dread (+ *inf.*)
torpeo (2): to be struck motionless
turba, -ae *f.*: a mob
vesper, vesperis *m.*: evening
victoria, -ae *f.*: victory
virtus, virtutis *f.*: strength, power

---

avibus: abl. of association, "with birds"
metu: abl. of means, "with fear"
de vespero: "takes its name *from evening*" i.e. the bat (*vespertilio*)
viribus...monitu: abl. after *implet*, "the king fills them *with strength and warning*"
metu: abl. of means, "strick motionless *from fear*"

Amplexatur aves ulnis victoria laetis;

    Pro titulo poenam transfuga sumit avis:

Vellere nuda suo, pro plumis vellera vestit

    Edictumque subit ne nisi nocte volet.

Non bonus est civis qui praefert civibus hostem:

    Utiliter servit nemo duobus eris.

amplexor (1): to embrace, clasp
bonus, -a, -um: good, honest
civis, civis *m./f.*: fellow citizen
edictum, -i *n.*: a proclamation, edict
erus, eri *m.*: a master, owner
hostis, -is *m/f.*: an enemy
laetus, -a, -um: joyful
nudus, -a, -um: nude, bare
pluma, -ae *f.*: a feather, plume
poena, -ae *f.*: a penalty, punishment
praefero: prefer X (*acc.*) over Y (*dat.*)

servio (4): to serve (+ *dat.*)
subeo (4): go underneath, undergo, endure
sumo (3): to take
titulus, -i *m.*: a title, distinction
transfuga, -ae *f.*: a deserter
ulna, -ae *f.*: an arm
utiliter: usefully
vellus, velleris *n.*: fleece, hide
vestio (4): to clothe, put on
volo (1): to fly

ulnis laetis: abl. of manner, "embraces *with joyful arms*"
pro titulo: "instead of distinction"
vellere suo: abl. of separation after nuda, "nude of *her proper fleece*" (i.e. her feathers)
vellera: "he wears *the hides*" i.e. he receives blows from others
ne volet: pres. subj. in indirect prohibition, "an edict *not to fly*"
duobus eris: dat. after servit, "serve *two masters*"

Fable 45: De filomena et accipitre

A hawk attacks a swallow's nest, and the mother begins to plead with the hawk to save her young. The hawk concedes, and tells the swallow to sing her lovely song for him. The swallow sings, although she feels hatred for the hawk in her heart; the hawk must notice this, for he says that the song is vulgar, and kills all of the young, with the mother looking on. The fable devotes an entire four lines to lamenting the misfortunes of the mother, who would have rather died than lose her young. In the last lines of the fable, however, justice is served, as the hawk is trapped by a fowler. The moral points out that an evil way of life deserves an evil end; although, notably, this doesn't account for the swallow's loss.

Dum filomena sedet, studium movet oris amoenum,

    Sic sibi, sic nido visa placere suo.

Impetit accipiter nidum: pro pignore mater

    Supplicat; alter ait: "Plus prece carmen amo.

Nec prece pretio, sed amoeno flectere cantu

    Me potes." ille silet, dulcius illa canit.

---

accipiter, accipitris *m./f.*: a hawk
amo (1): to love
amoenus, -a, -um: beautiful
cano (3): to sing
cantus, cantus *m.*: a song
carmen, carminis *n.*: a song, music
dulcior, -us: pleasant, sweet
filomena, -ae *f.*: a nightingale
flecto (3): to bend, persuade
impeto (3): to attack, assail
mater, matris *f.*: a mother
moveo (2): to move, stir, agitate

nidus, -i *m.*: a nest
os, oris *n.*: a mouth, speech
pignus, pignoris *n.*: a hostage
placeo (2): to please, satisfy
plus (*adv.*): more
pretium, -i *n.*: a price, value
prex, precis *f.*: a prayer, request
sedeo (2): to sit, settle
sileo (2): to be silent
studium, -i *n.*: eagerness, enthusiasm
supplico (1): to pray
video (2) **vidi, visus**: see, look at

studium ... amoenum: "moves the sweet enthusiasm," i.e. she sings
prece: abl. of comparison after *plus*, "more than *prayer*"
prece pretio: abl. of means, *hendiadys*, "not to persuade *with a valuable prayer*"

Mente gemit, licet ore canat, mens eius acescit,

Cuius mellifluum manat ab ore melos.

Impia fatur avis: "Sordet modus iste canoris."

Et laniat natum, matre vidente, suum.

Mater obit, nec obire potest: sic vivit, ut ipsam

Vincat vita necem, plus nece cladis habens.

Cor matris patitur plus nati corpore: corpus

Rodit avis rostro, cor fodit ense dolor.

---

acesco (3): to turn sour
canor, canoris *m.*: a song
clades, cladis *f.*: defeat
cor, cordis *n.*: a heart
corpus, corporis *n.*: a body
fodio (3): to dig, dig out
for (1): to speak, talk
gemo (3): to moan, groan
impius, -a, -um: wicked, impious
lanio (1): to tear, mangle
licet (2): to it is permitted
mano (1): to flow, pour
mellifluus, -a, -um: sweet flowing

melos, -i *n.*: a song
mens, mentis *f.*: mind
modus, -i *m.*: a manner, mode
natus, -i *m.*: a son, child
nex, necis *f.*: death, murder
obeo, obire: die
patior (3): to suffer
plus, pluris *(gen.)*: more
rodo (3): to gnaw, peck
rostrum, -i *n.*: a beak
sordeo (2): to be dirty, vulgar
vinco (3): to conquer, defeat
vita, -ae *f.*: life, career

---

mente ... ore: abl. of place, "in the mind ... in the mouth" an *antithesis*"
canat: pres. subj. concessive after licet, "although she sings"
mellifluum ... melos: "sweet-flowing song" *figura etymologica*
matre vidente: abl. abs., "with the mother watching"
suum: reflexive pronoun where *eius* would be expected
ut...vincat: pres. subj. in purpose clause, "*in order* that life *conquer* death"
nece ... corpore: abl. of comparison after *plus*, "having more of defeat *than death*"
corpore: abl. of comparison after *plus*, "suffers *more than the body* of the child"
rostro ... ense: abl. of means, "gnaws *with his beak ... with a sword*" i.e. like a sword
  (which is sharper than the beak)

Vestigat sua poena scelus: nam, fraudibus uso

Aucupe, fraudosam viscus inescat avem.

Fine malo claudi mala vita meretur: iniquus,

Qua capit insontes, se dolet arte capi.

ars, artis *f.*: skill, art, trick
auceps, aucupis *m.*: a bird-catcher, fowler
capio (3): to take hold, seize
claudo (3): to close, shut
claudus, -a, -um: defective
doleo (2): to hurt, feel pain
dolor, doloris *m.*: pain, anguish
ensis, ensis *m.*: a sword
finis, finis *m./f.*: an end
fraus, fraudis *f.*: fraud, trickery
inesco (1): to entice, fill with food

iniquus, a, -um: unjust, unfair
insons, insontis (*gen.*): guiltless, innocent
malum, -i *n.*: evil
mereo (2): to earn, deserve
poena, -ae *f.*: a penalty, punishment
scelus, sceleris *n.*: a crime
utor (3): to use
vestigo (1): to track down, search for
viscus, -i *m.*: bird-lime (used for trapping birds)

uso aucupe: abl. abs., "the fowler having used" +abl.
fraudibus: abl. after *uso*, "used *trickery*"
fine malo: abl. of means, "closed *by a bad end*"
claudi: pres. pass. inf. after *meretur*, "deserves *to be closed*"
qua: abl. with antecedent *arte*, "captured by the art *by which*"
capi: pres. pass. inf. after *dolet*, "grieves that he *is captured*"

Fable 46: De lupo et vulpe

Here the two villains meet again, but this time the fox is not so honest as in the other fable by the same name. The fox is envious of the prey that the wolf has caught and speaks sweetly to the wolf, trying to score a share for herself. The wolf sees through the fox's disguise and refuses to share his catch. The fox, sorely disappointed, finds the shepherd, and tells him the location of the wolf's den, so that he is able to slay the wolf. The fox is then able to devour the wolf's hoard, but her joy is short lived, as she falls into a snare but an hour later. The moral of this fable is not unlike the previous fable in cautioning that an envious man will bring harm unto himself.

Ditat praeda lupum; ducit lupus otia longo

Fausta cibo. Vulpes invidet, ista movet:

"Frater, ave. Miror cur tanto tempore mecum

Non fueris; nequeo non memor esse tui."

Ille refert: "Pro me vigilet tua cura, precari

Numina non cesses, ne mea vita ruat.

---

cesso (1): to be remiss, cease from
cibus, -i *m.*: food
cura, -ae *f.*: concern, worry
dito (1): to enrich
duco (3): to lead, command
faustus, -a, -um: favorable
frater, fratris *m.*: a brother
invideo (2): to envy
longus, -a, -um: long
lupus, lupi *m.*: a wolf
memor, memoris (*gen.*): remembering (+ *gen.*)

miro (1): to be amazed, surprised
nequeo, (4): be unable, cannot (+ *inf.*)
numen, numinis *n.*: divine will
otium, -i *n.*: leisure, spare time
praeda, -ae *f.*: booty, loot
precor (1): to beg, implore
refero, referre: to respond
ruo (3): to destroy, ruin
tantus, a, um: of such size, so great
vigilo (1): to remain awake, be awake
vulpes, vulpis *f.*: a fox

---

longo cibo: abl. of cause, "from the long food" an example of transfered epithet since the longo more properly goes with otia

tanto tempore: abl. of time within which, "for such a great time" where we would expect an accusative

cur...non fueris: perf. subj. in indirect question, "wonder why you have not been"

nequeo non: "I am not able to not be mindful" i.e. I can't forget

vigilet: pres. subj. jussive, "let your care stay awake!"

non cesses: pres. subj. jussive, "may you not cease" +inf.

ne...ruat: pres. subj. in noun clause after *precari*, "pray that my life *not be destroyed*"

Fraude tamen munita venis falsoque venenum

    Melle tegis. Dolor est copia nostra tibi.

Extorquere paras aliquid furtumque minaris,

    Sed mea furtivam respuit esca gulam."

Spreta redit; spretam stimulat dolor; apta dolori

    Fraus subit: ad pecorum transvolat illa ducem.

Hunc monet his verbis: "Tua gratia muneris instar

    Sit mihi, namque lupum dat mea cura tibi.

Hostem perde tuum: tuto jacet hostis in antro."

---

antrum, -i *n.*: a cave, cavern
aptus, -a, -um: suitable, adapted
copia, -ae *f.*: plenty, abundance
dux, ducis *m.*: a leader, guide
esca, -ae *f.*: food, meat
extorqueo (2): to extort, tear away
falsus, -a, -um: wrong, false
faveo (2): to favor, oblige
furtivus, -a, -um: stolen, secret
furtum, -i *n.*: theft, trick
gratia, -ae *f.*: favor, thanks
gula, -ae *f.*: a throat, neck
hostis, -is *m/f.*: an enemy
instar: as large as (+ *gen.*)
jaceo (2): to lie, lie down
mel, mellis *n.*: honey, sweetness
minor (1): to threaten
moneo (2): to remind, advise, warn

munio (4) **munivi, munitus**: fortify, arm
munus, muneris *n.*: service, duty
namque: on the other hand
paro (1): to prepare (+ *inf.*)
pecus, pecoris *n.*: a herd, flock
perdo (3): to ruin, destroy
redeo, redire: return, retire
respuo (3): to reject, spit, spew out
sperno (3) **sprevi, spretus**: scorn, despise
stimulo (1): to incite, rouse to frenzy
subeo, subire: arise, comes from below
tego (3): to cover, protect
transvolo (1): to fly across
tutus, -a, -um: safe, prudent
venenum, -i *n.*: poison, drug
venio (4): to come
verbum, -i *n.*: a word, proverb
vir, -i *m.*: a man

---

munita: perf. part. nom., "you, *having been armed* with fraud"
falso melle: abl. of means, "cover *with false sweetness*"
dolor: nom. pred., "our abundance is *grief*"
furtivam gulam: a stolen throat, i.e. a throat intending to steal, transferred epithet
spreta: perf. part. nom., "she, *having been scorned*"
dolori: dat. after *apta*, "suitable *to her pain*"
pecorum ducem: the leader of the flocks, i.e. a shepherd
sit: pres. subj. jussive, "*let* your thanks *be*"
tuto in antro: "in a safe cave" transferred epithet

Vir favet: antra petit, hic necat ense lupum.

Ista lupi consumit opes, sed floret ad horam

Vita nocens. Vulpes, casse retenta, gemit:

"Cur nocui? Nocet ecce mihi nocuisse nocivo.

Jure cado, cuius concidit arte lupus."

Vivere de rapto vitam rapit: invidus, instans

Alterius damnis, in sua damna redit.

---

alter, -a, -um: one (of two)
ars, artis *f.*: art, skill
cado (3): to fall, sink
cassis, cassis *n.*: a hunting net
concido (3) **concidi**: to die
consumo (3): to burn up, destroy
damnum, -i *n.*: damage, harm
floreo (2): to flourish, bloom
gemo (3): to moan, groan
hora, -ae *f.*: an hour, time
instans, instantis (*gen.*): eager for (+ *dat.*)
invidus, -a, -um: hateful

jus, juris *n.*: law, right
lupus, lupi *m.*: a wolf
neco (1): to kill, murder
nocens, nocentis (*gen.*): harmful, guilty
noceo (2) **nocui**: harm, hurt
nocivus, -a, -um: harmful, injurious
ops, opis *f.*: wealth
peto (3): to attack, seek
rapio (3): to drag off, snatch
raptum, -i *n.*: plunder
retineo (2) **retinui, retentus**: to hold back, restrain
vivo (3): to be alive, live

---

muneris instar: "as large as my service"
ista: i.e. the fox
ad horam: "blooms *up to an hour*"
retenta: perf. part. nom., "she, *having been caught* by a net"
nocuisse: perf. inf. after impersonal nocet, "it harms *to have harmed*" note the *polyptoton*
jure: abl. of manner, "I fall *justly*"
mihi ... novivo: dat., "harms *harmful me*"
vivere: subj. of *rapit*, "*to live* from plunder plunders life"
alterius: gen. of *alter*, "the harm *of another*"

Fable 47: De cervo, tibiis, et cornibus

Here is another common fable in the elegiac Romulus: a stag sees the reflection of his antlers in a pool, which gladdens him. He then looks down and notices his legs, which are very thin, and scorns their weakness. A pack of dogs begins to chase him, and he runs away, but is soon trapped in a tree by his horns. The end of the fable notes that his legs, which he had shamed, would have been his escape, while the horns that he was so proud of ensnared him and brought upon his death. The moral notes the foolishness of scorning anything that might be of benefit. The woodcut that both Steinhowel and Caxton use to correspond to this fable is particularly interesting-- you will see that there is a man playing a pipe leading the dogs, even though no such character appears in the fable. The language in the fable however does describe his legs as "tibia macra pedum," or the "thin flutes of his feet." It seems that the flute in the image may not have been meant to depict a part of the fable at all, but instead as a kind of visual mnemonic to signal to the reader that it was his pipe-like legs which could have been the key to the stag's freedom.

Fons nitet, argento similis. Sitis arida cervum

Huc rapit; haurit aquas, se speculatur aquis.

Hunc beat; hunc mulcet ramosae gloria frontis;

Hunc premit, hunc laedit tibia macra pedum.

Ecce canes, tonat ira canum; timet ille, timenti

---

aqua, -ae *f.*: water
argentum, -i *n.*: silver
aridus, -a -um: dry, parched
beo (1): to bless
canis, canis *m/f.*: a dog, hound
cervus, -i *m.*: a stag, deer
cornu, cornus *n.*: a horn
fons, fontis *m.*: a spring, fountain
frons, frontis *m./f.*: a forehead
gloria, -ae *f.*: glory, fame
haurio (4): to drink, swallow, drain
ira, -ae *f.*: anger, ire
laedo (3): to hurt, embarass

macer, -ra, -rum: thin
mulceo (2): to appease, please
niteo (2): to shine, glitter
pes, pedis *m.*: a foot
premo (3): to press, overwhelm
ramosus, -a, -um: having many branches
rapio (3): to snatch, catch
sitis, sitis *f.*: thirst
speculor (1): to watch, observe
tibia, -ae *f.*: a leg, flute
timeo (2): to fear, dread
tono (1): to thunder

---

argento: dat. after *similis*, "like *silver*"
hunc ... hunc: anaphora

Fit fuga: culpati cruris adorat opem.

Silvae claustra subit, cornu retinente moratur:

Crure neci raptum cornua longa necant.

Spernere quod prosit et amare quod obsit ineptum est.

Prodest quod fugimus et quod amamus obest.

adoro (1): to beg
amo (1): to love
claustrum, **-i** *n.*: an enclosure
crus, **cruris** *n.*: a leg, shank (of a tree)
culpo (1): to blame, find fault with
fuga, **-ae** *f.*: a flight, fleeing
fugio (3): to flee, avoid
ineptus, **-a**, **-um**: silly, foolish
longus, **-a**, **-um**: long, tall

moro (1): to delay
nex, **necis** *f.*: death
obsum, **obsesse**: to hurt
ops, **opis** *f.*: power, might
prosum, **prodesse**: to be useful
retineo (2): to hold back, restrain
silva, **-ae** *f.*: wood, forest
subeo (4): go, move underneath

culpati: perf. part. agreeing with *cruris*, "power *of the faulted* leg"

cornu retinente: abl. abs., "with the horn holding back"

crure: abl. of means, "caught *by a tree shank*" note the pun on *crus*, which is somewhat forced because presumably his horns would be caught by the branches, not the "shank" of the tree

neci: dat. of purpose, "snatched *for death*"

spernere...amare: inf. subject of *est*, "*to spurn... to love* is foolish"

quod prosit...quod obsit: pres. subj. in relative clause of characteristic, "that which is useful...that which harms"

Fable 48: De viro et uxore

Better known as the widow of Ephesus, the story in this fable is more familiar from its apearance in the *Satyricon* of Petronius. The fable here is told just as the earlier story; a widow is mourning over the body of her husband when she is seen by a soldier who is guarding the body of a thief on a cross. The soldier finds himself captivated by the widow, but while he is pouring out his love to her, the thief's body is taken off the cross. The soldier laments that he will surely be sent into exile for this, but the wife strategizes that the body of her husband might substitute for the thief's missing body. This tale is used by Petronius, and by countless others, to point out the fickleness of a woman's love, and this version is no different; the woman is chastised in the moral for oppressing men with fear and pain. Later versions of the fable, beginning with Marie de France, praise the ingenuity of the widow and approve her logic of using her dead husband's body, which is a useless corpse, to prevent the death of another.

Dum vir et uxor amant, uxorem privat amato

Parca viro, nec eam privat amore viri.

Conjugis amplectens tumulum, pro conjuge vexat

Ungue genas, oculos fletibus, ora sono.

---

amor, amoris *m.*: love, affection
amplector (3): to surround, embrace
conjunx, -conjugis *m.*: a spouse
fletus, fletus *m.*: crying, tears
gena, -ae *f.*: cheeks, eyes
oculus, -i *m.*: an eye
os, oris *n.*: a mouth, speech
Parca, -ae *f.*: Fate

privo (1): to deprive, rob, free
sonus, -i *m.*: a noise, sound
tumulus, -i *m.*: a mound, tomb
unguis, -is *m.*: a fingernail
uxor, uxoris *f.*: a wife
vexo (1): to shake, torment
vir, -i *m.*: a man, husband

---

amato viro ... amore: abl. separation after *privat*, "deprives her *of beloved husband ...* but not *her love*" i.e. she still loves him after losing him

viri: gen. objective, "love *for her husband*"

ungue ... fletibus ... sono: abl. of means, "torments *with her nail ... with tears ... with sound*"

110

Hanc juvat ipse dolor, nequit haec de sede revelli

Grandine seu tenebris seu prece sive minis.

Ecce reum damnat judex: crux horrida punit,

In cruce custodit tempore noctis eques.

Hic sitit; ad tumulum vocat hunc et clamor et ignis:

Oratque aquae munus; haec dat et ille bibit.

aegrum nectareis audet cor inungere verbis;

Hunc vocat ad primum cura timoris opus.

Sed redit et dulces monitus intexit amaro

Cordi: victa subit castra doloris amor.

---

aeger, -ra, -rum: sick
amarus, -a, -um: bitter
aqua, -ae *f.*: water
audeo (2): to intend, dare
bibo (3): to drink
castrum, -i *n.*: a fort, fortress
clamor, clamoris *m.*: a shout, war-cry
cor, cordis *n.*: heart, mind
crux, crucis *f.*: a cross
cura, -ae *f.*: anxiety
custodio (4): to guard
damno (1): to pass judgment, find guilty
dolor, doloris *m.*: pain, anguish
dulcis, dulce: pleasant, sweet
eques, equitis *m.*: a horseman, knight
grando, grandinis *f.*: hail, hail-storm
horridus, -a, -um: horrible
ignis, ignis *m.*: fire, passion
intexo (3): to weave in
inungo (3): to anoint
judex, judicis *m.*: a judge, juror
juvat (1): to it pleases, delights

mina, -ae *f.*: threats, menaces
monitus, monitus *m.*: warning, advice
nectareus, -a, -um: sweet as nectar
nequeo (4): be unable, cannot
nox, noctis *f.*: night
opus, operis *n.*: duty, work
oro (1): to beg, ask for
prex, precis *f.*: prayer, request
primus, -a, -um: first
punio (4): to punish
redeo (4): return, go back
reus, -i *m.*: a culprit, guilty party
revello (3): to tear, pull away
sedes, sedis *f.*: a seat
sitio (4): to be thirsty
tempus, temporis *n.*: time
tenebra, t-ae *f.*: darkness
timor, timoris *m.*: fear
verbum, -i *n.*: a word, proverb
vinco (3), **vici, victus**: to conquer
voco (1): to call

---

revelli: pres. inf. pass. after *nequit*, "refuses *to be pulled away*"
crux punit: "the cross punishes" i.e. he is condemned to the cross, transferred epithet
tempore noctis: (= *nocte*) "at night"
cura: nom. subject, *"the anxiety* of fear calls"
amaro cordi: dat after *intexit*, "weaves advice into *her bitter heart*"
victa castra: *"the conquered fortress* of grief" an example of *prolepsis*

Vir, metuens furi furem, suspendia furis
  Visit, sed viduam, tactus amore, petit.
Hanc ligat amplexu fructumque ligurit amoris.
  Hinc redit ad furem, sed loca fure carent.
Hic dolet, hoc questu dolor hic instigat amicam:
  "Non bene servato fure, timore premor.
Rex mihi servandum dederat: me regius ensis
  Terret et extorrem me jubet esse timor."

---

amica, -ae *f.*: a girl-friend
amplexus, amplexus *m.*: a clasp, embrace
careo (2): to be without (+ *abl.*)
doleo (2): to hurt
ensis, ensis *m.*: a sword
extorris, -e: exiled
fructus, fructus *m.*: crops, fruit
fur, furis *m./f.*: a thief, robber
instigo (1): to urge on, stir
jubeo (2): to order, command
ligo (1): to bind, fasten
ligurio (4): to desire, taste
locum, -i *n.*: a seat, place

metuo (3): to fear, be afraid
peto (3): to attack
premo (3): to press, pursue
questus, -us *m.*: a complaint
regius, -a, -um: royal, of a king
rex, regis *m.*: a king
servo (1): to watch over
subeo, -ire:: to approach, attack
suspendium, -i *n.*: a hanging
tango (3) **tetigi, tactus**: to touch
terreo (2): to frighten, scare
viduus, -a, -um: widowed
viso (3): to visit, go to see

---

furi: dat. of advantage, "fearing a thief *for the thief*" i.e. that someone would steal the thief's body, which in fact happens
ligat ... ligurit: "*he binds ... he tastes*" note the pun
fure: abl. of specification after *carent*, "lack *the thief*" note the *polyptoton*
questu: abl. of means, "stirs her *with this complaint*"
servato fure: abl. abs., "the thief having been guarded"
sevandum: supine acc. expressing purpose, "had given him *in order to be guarded*"
extorrem: acc. pred., "orders me to be *exiled*"

Haec ait: "Inveni, quae spem tibi suscitet, artem.

Vir meus implebit in cruce furis onus."

Ipsa viri bustum reserat, pro fure catenat

Ipsa virum, restem subligat ipsa viro.

Huic merito succumbit eques; succumbit amori

Illa novo, ligat hos firmus amore torus.

Sola premit vivosque metu poenaque sepultos

Femina: femineum nil bene finit opus.

---

ars, **artis** *f.*: a device
bustum, **-i** *n.*: a tomb
cateno (1): to chain, bind
femina, **-ae** *f.*: a woman, female
femineus, **-a**, **-um**: woman's, female
finio (4): to limit, end
firmus, **-a**, **-um**: firm, steady
impleo (2): to satisfy, fulfill
invenio (4), **inveni**: to come upon
ligo (1): to bind, unite
merito: (*adv.*) rightly
metus, metus *m.*: fear, anxiety
nil: nothing

novus, **-a**, **-um**: new, fresh
onus, oneris *n.*: a load, burden
poena, **-ae** *f.*: a penalty, punishment
resero (1): to open up, unseal
restis, restis *f.*: a rope, cord
sepelio (4) **sepelivi, sepultus**: to bury
solus, **-a**, **-um**: only, alone
spes, spei *f.*: hope
subligo (1): to fasten X (*acc.*) to Y (*dat.*).
succumbo (3): to yield to (+ *dat.*)
suscito (1): to encourage, stir up
torus, **-i** *m.*: a wedding bed
vivus, **-a**, **-um**: alive, living

---

quae suscitet: pres. subj. in relative clause of characteristic, "device *which would raise*"
viro: dat. after *subligat*, "she ties a cord *to her husband*"
huic ... amori novo: dat. after succumbit, "he yields *to her* ... she *to a new love*"
amore: abl. of specification, "firm *with love*"
vivosque ... sepultos : (sc. *viros*) acc., "oppresses men *living ... and dead*"
metu poenaque: abl. of means, "oppresses *with fear and punishment*"
nil: indec., "ends well *not at all*"

Fable 49: De juvene et Thaide

Continuing the theme of the previous fable, here women are again presented in a negative light. Thais ensnares young men with her wiles, and then receives all she wants from them by promising them true love. Thais preforms her tricks on a particular young man who is familiar with her ways; he tells the woman that he would be happy to return her love, except that he fears to be deceived by her wicked tongue. The moral further incriminates Thais by saying that she lacks love itself, only caring for the gifts of love.

Arte sua Thais juvenes irretit: amorem

    Fingit et ex ficto fructus amore venit.

A multis fert multa procis; ex omnibus unum

    Eligit, huic veri spondet amoris opes.

"Sum tua sisque meus cupio; plus omnibus unum

    Te volo, sed nolo munus habere tuum."

Percipit ille dolos et reddit qualia sumpsit:

    "Sis mea simque tuus. Nos decet equus amor;

Vivere non vellem nisi mecum vivere velles:

    Tu mihi sola salus, tu mihi sola quies;

---

ars, artis *f.*: skill, art, trick
cupio (3): to wish, long for, desire
eligo (3): to pick out, choose
fero, ferre: to bring, bear
fingo (3) finxi, fictus: to mold, form, shape
habeo (2): to have
irretio (4): to entangle, catch in a net
juvenis, juvenis *m./f.*: a young man
multus, -a, -um: much, many
munus, muneris *n.*: service, gift
nolo, nolle: wish not to

ops, opis *f.*: wealth
plus (*adv.*): more (+ *abl.*)
procus, -i *m.*: a wooer, suitor
spondeo (2): to promise X (*acc.*) to Y (*dat.*)
Thais, Thaidis *f.*: Thais, a famous Greek courtesan whose name became generic for a courtesan
unus, -a, -um: alone
venio (4): to come
verus, -a, -um: true
volo, velle: wish, want

---

fert multa: "she takes many gifts"
sis: pres. subj. in noun clause after *cupio*, "I desire *that you be* mine"
plus omnibus: "I want you alone *more than all*"

114

Sed falli timeo, quia me tua lingua fefellit.

Preteriti ratio scire futura facit.

Vitat avis taxum quam, gustu teste, probavit.

Fallere vult hodie, si qua fefellit heri."

Thaida si quis amat, sua, non se, credat amari:

Thais amore caret, munus amantis amat.

---

aequus, -a, -um: equal, reciprocal	**probo** (1): to try, examine
avis, avis *f.*: a bird	**quies, quietis** *f.*: quiet, calm
careo (2): to be without (+ *abl.*)	**ratio, rationis** *f.*: an account
credo (3): to trust, entrust	**reddo** (3): to return, restore
decet (2): it is fitting	**salus, salutis** *f.*: health
dolus, doli *m.*: a trick, device	**scio** (4): know, understand
fallo (3), **fefelli**: to deceive	**solus, -a, -um**: only
futurus, -a, -um: about to be, future	**sumo** (3) **sumpsi**: to take up, begin
gustus, gustus *m.*: tasting, appetite	**taxus, -i** *f.*: a yew-tree
heri: yesterday	**testis, testis** *m.*: a witness
hodie: today	**timeo** (2): to fear, dread
lingua, -ae *f.*: a tongue, speech	**vito** (1): to avoid, evade
percipio (3): to perceive	**vivo** (3): to be alive, live
praeteritum, -i *n.*: the past	

sis ... sim: pres. subj. in hortatory and jussive clauses, "*may you be* mine ... *may I be* yours"

vellem ... velles: impf. subj. in present contrafactual condition, "*I would not wish ... unless you would wish*"

falli: pres.inf. pass., "fear *to be deceived*"

scire: pres. inf. after causative *facit*, "causes *to know*"

gustu teste: abl. abs., "with taste as a witness"

si qua: abl. of manner, "if in any way"

sua, non se: acc. subj. of *amari* in ind. st. after *credat*, "believe *his own things, not himself* to be loved"

credat: pres. subj. in future less vivid apodosis, "he would believe"

Fable 50: De patre et filio

Like the early "Woman Marrying a Thief," the narrative of the father and the son serves as a framework for the animal fable. Here a father is frustrated with his son's bad behavior, but continuously punishes his servants for it. The fable is included to instruct the old man; a wise man hooks both an ox and his calf to a yoke, so that the calf might learn to plow from his parent. The moral suggests to the father this form of instruction—teaching by example.

Est pater, huic natus; hic patri cedere nescit:

    Nam fugienda facit et facienda fugit.

Mens vaga discurrit et menti consonat aetas:

    Mentis et aetatis turbine frena fugit.

Ira senis punit pro nati crimine servos.

    Instruit ista senem fabula nota seni.

Cauta bovem vitulumque manus supponit aratro:

---

aetas, aetatis *f.*: lifetime, age
aratrum, aratri *n.*: a plow
bos, bovis *m.*: an ox, bull
cautus, -a, -um: cautious, careful
cedo (3): to yield, submit
consono (1): to sound, utter
crimen, criminis *n.*: a sin, crime
discurro (3): to wander, roam
fabula, -ae *f.*: a story, tale
filius, -i *m.*: a son
frenum, -i *n.*: a bridle, check
fugio (3): to flee
instruo (3): to prepare, instruct
ira, -ae *f.*: anger, ire

manus, manus *f.*: a hand
mens, mentis *f.*: mind, reason
natus, -i *m.*: a son, child
nescio (4): to not know how to (+ *inf.*)
notus, -a, -um: well known, familiar
pater, patris *m.*: a father
punio (4): to punish
senex, senis *m.*: an old man
servus, -i *m.*: a slave, servant
suppono (3): to place X (*acc.*) under Y (*dat.*)
turbo, turbinis *n.*: a whirlwind, storm
vagus, -a, -um: roving, wandering
vitulus, -i *m.*: a calf

---

patri: dat. after *cedere*, "yield *to the father*"

fugienda ... facienda: gerundives, "things to be fled ... things to be done"

menti: dat. after *consonat*, "conforms *to the mind*"

turbine: abl. of cause, "*because of the storm* of his mind and age"

pro nati crimine: it was not uncommon in antiquity to punish servants for the crime of their master

seni: dat. after *nota*, "known *to the old man*"

cauta ... manus: nom. subject, "*a cautious hand* plans"

aratro: dat. after *supponit*, "places under *the plow*"

Hic subit, ille jugum pellit. Arator ait:

"Gaude, laetus ara, tu quem domat usus arandi.

A bove majori discat arare minor.

Non placet ut sudes, sed des exempla minori,

Qui pede, qui cornu, pugnat abire jugo."

Sic domat indomitum domito bove cautus arator,

Sic veterem sequitur junior ille bovem.

Proficit exempli merito cautela docendi,

Majorique sua credat in arte minor.

---

arator, aratoris *m.*: a plowman, farmer
aro (1): to plow, till
cautela, -ae *f.*: caution, precaution
cornu, cornus *n.*: a horn, hoof
disco (3): to learn to (+ *inf.*)
doceo (2): to teach, show
domo (1): to subdue, master
exemplum, -i *n.*: an example
gaudeo (2): to be glad, rejoice
indomitus, -a, -um: untamed
jugum, jugi *n.*: a yoke
junior, junius: younger
laetus, -a, -um: happy, joyful

major, -us: larger, greater
meritum, -i *n.*: merit, service
minor, -us: inferior in rank
pello (3): to beat, resist
pes, pedis *m.*: a foot
placeo (2): to please, satisfy
proficio (3): to accomplish, be useful
pugno (1): to fight, dispute (+ *inf.*)
sequor (3): to follow
subeo (4): go/move underneath
sudo (1): to sweat, perspire
utor (3): to use
veterrimus, -a, -um: old, aged

---

arandi: gerund gen., "the use *of plowing* masters"

discat: pres. subj. jussive, "*let a small one learn* to plow"

ut sudes: pres subj in noun clause after *placet*, "it does not please you *to sweat*"

des: pres. subj. jussive, "you ought to give"

jugo: dat. after *abire*, "to endure *the yoke*"

domito bove: abl. abs., "while taming the cow"

merito: abl. of manner, "is *deservedly* useful"

docendi: gerundive agreeing with *exempli*, "of the example *that must be taught*" i.e. teaching by example

credat: pres. subj. jussive, "let the lesser trust" + dat.

Fable 51: De vipera et lima

In this fable, not only do animals have the ability to speak, but inanimate objects suddenly are able to discern good from evil as well. A viper begins to gnaw on a file that she found in a workman's shop. The file speaks to the viper, explaining that her bite is stronger than the viper's, and that she is able to turn hard materials into dust. The moral doesn't truly address either character, but notes that the strong should love other things which are strong, while the smaller should fear those with strength.

Vipera fabrilem, dapis anxia, tendit in aedem;

Incipit haec limam rodere, lima loqui:

"Nescis posse meum, quae sit mea gloria nescis:

Dente meo pateris. Non ego dente tuo.

In tenuem ferrum forti molo dente farinam,

Et cadit attritu dura farina meo.

---

aedis, -is *f.*: a dwelling
anxius, -a, -um: anxious about (+ *gen.*)
attritus, -us *m.*: rubbing
cado (3): to fall, sink
daps, dapis *f.*: a feast
dens, dentis *m.*: a tooth
durus, -a, -um: hard, rough
fabrilis, -e: of a workman
farina, -ae *f.*: flour, dust
ferrum, -i *n.*: iron
fortis, forte: strong

gloria, -ae *f.*: glory, fame
incipio (3): to begin, start
lima, -ae *f.*: a file
loquor (3): to speak, say
molo (3): to grind
nescio (3): to not know
patior (3): to suffer, undergo
rodo (3): to gnaw, peck
tendo (3): to stretch, spread
tenuis, tenue: thin, fine
vipera, -ae *f.*: a viper, snake

loqui (sc. incipit): pres. inf., "the file (begins) *to speak*"
posse: inf. used as a substantive, "know my *power*"
quae sit: pres subj. in ind. quest. after *nescis*, "know *what is* my glory"
in tenuem ... farinam: "grind iron *into fine flour*"
attritu meo: abl. means., "*by my rubbing*"

118

Ferrea mordaci castigo tubera morsu,

    Aspera plano, seco longa, foranda foro.

Deliras, igitur, cum dente minaris inermi.

    Rideo, quod ferior; vulnera ferre gemis."

Fortem fortis amet: nam fortem fortior angit.

    Maiori timeat obvius ire minor.

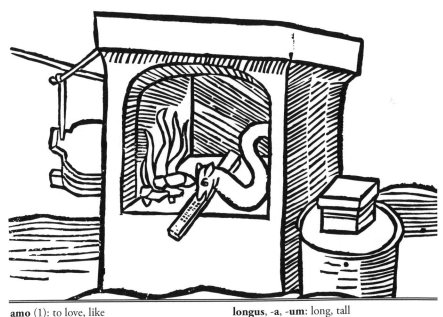

amo (1): to love, like
ango (3): to choke, strangle, cause pain
asperus, -a, -um: uneven, rough
castigo (1): to correct, smooth
deliro (1): to be mad, crazy
ferio (4): to hit, strike
fero, ferre: bring, bear
ferreus, -a, -um: made of iron
foro (1): to pierce, bore
gemo (3): to moan, grieve (+ *inf.*)
igitur: therefore
inermus, -a, -um: unarmed, defenseless

longus, -a, -um: long, tall
major, -us: greater, larger
minor (1): to threaten
minus, -or: less, smaller
mordax, mordacis (*gen.*): biting
morsus, morsus *m.*: a bite
obvius, -a, -um: in the way of (+ *dat.*)
plano (1): to level, flatten
rideo (2): to laugh at
seco (1): to cut, sever
tuber, tuberis *n.*: a protuberance, bump
vulnus, vulneris *n.*: a wound

foranda: neut. pl. gerundive, "I bore *the things that must be bored*
amet: pres. subj. jussive, "let the strong love"
timeat: pres. subj. jussive," *let the smaller fear* to go"

Fable 52: De lupis et ovibus

The wolves are engaged in a battle with the sheep, and with the help of the dog and the ram, the sheep seem to be winning. The wolves loose hope, turning to deceit instead. The wolf and the ram negotiate a treaty, which is marked by the exchange of hostages. The sheep trade the dog, while the wolves trade their young. This agreement holds until the young wolves grow up; the treaty is then soon forgotten and the wolves devour the sheep. The moral warns against loosing a defender as the sheep did, saying that without a strong defense you are vulnerable to the enemy.

Pugna lupis opponit oves, oviumque satelles

   Est canis, est vervex: haec ope fidit ovis.

Palma diu dormit, desperat turba luporum

   Et, simulans foedus, foedere temptat ovem.

Foedus utrumque fides jurato numine fulcit,

   Id lupus, id simplex obside firmat ovis,

---

cane, canis *n.*: a dog, hound
despero (1): to despair
dormio (4): to sleep, rest
fides, fidei *f.*: faith
fido (3): to trust (in) (+ *abl.*)
firmo (1): to support, confirm
foedo (3): to pollute
foedus, foederis *n.*: a treaty, pledge
fulcio (4): to prop up, support
juro (1): to swear
lupus, -i *m.*: a wolf
numen, numinis *n.*: divine will, divinity
obses, obsidis *m./f.*: a hostage

oppono (3): to oppose, place opposite
ops, opis *f.*: help
ovis, ovis *f.*: a sheep
palma, -ae *f.*: palm award, victory
pugna, pugnae *f.*: a battle, fight
satelles, satellitis *m./f.*: an accomplice
simplex: simple, plain
simulo (1): to imitate, pretend
tempto (1): to test, bribe
turba, -ae *f.*: a crowd, mob
uterque, -a, um: each, either of two
vervex, vervis (**M**): wether

---

lupis: dat. after compound verb, "opposes the sheep *to the wolves*"
ovium ... canis: gen. of material, "accomplice consisting *of sheep and a dog*"
foedus, foedere: "pretending *a treaty*, they try *to pollute*" a pun
jurato numine: abl. abs., "a divinty having been sworn" i.e. an oath having been
   taken

Datque lupis, male sana, canes, recipitque luporum

    Pignora: nec metuit nec sua damna videt.

Cum natura jubet natos ululare lupinos,

    Turba lupina furit, foedera rupta querens.

Ergo pecus, tutoris egens, in viscera mergit:

    Praeside nuda suo sic tumulatur ovis.

Tutorem retinere suum tutissima res est:

    Nam si tutor abest, hostis obesse potest.

---

absum, abesse: absent, be lacking
damnum, damni *n.*: injury
egeo (2): to lack, want (+ *gen.*)
furo (3): to rave, rage
hostis, -is *m/f.*: an enemy
jubeo (2): to order, command
lupinus, -a, -um: of or belonging to a wolf
malus, -a, -um: bad, evil
mergo (3): to dip, plunge
metuo (3): to fear, be afraid
natura, -ae *f.*: nature
natus, -i *m.*: a child, children (pl.)
nudus, -a, -um: nude, stripped of (+ *abl.*)
obsum, obesse: to hurt

pecus, pecoris *n.*: a herd, flock
pignus, pignoris *n.*: a pledge
queror (3): to complain, protest
recipio (3): to recover
retineo (2): to retain, preserve
rumpo (3): to break, destroy
sanus, -a, -um: sound, healthy
tumulo (1): to bury
tutissimus, -a, -um: safe
tutor, tutoris *m.*: a protector, defender
ululo (1): to howl, yell
video (2): to see, look at
viscus, visceris *n.*: innards

---

male sane (= insana): "she, *madly*, gives"
luporum pignora: "receives *pledges of the wolves*" i.e. the wolves' pups as hostages
foedera rupta (sc. esse): ind. st. after *querens*, "protesting that the pledges have been broken"
in viscera mergit: "plunge into their stomachs" i.e. they are eaten by the wolves
praeside suo: abl. of separation after nuda, "stripped *from their own protector*"
retinere: pres. inf. subject of *est*, "*to keep* your protecter is safest"

121

Fable 53: De viro et securi

With a moral similar to the previous fable, here an ax-blade is without a handle, so it travels into the woods, asking a tree to supply a handle. The tree agrees, but soon the ax, equipped with a handle, is used to chop down the entire forest. The tree then laments his foolishness, and the readers are again reminded not to strengthen their enemy.

Quo teneatur eget nil ausa secare securis.

Armet eam lucus, vir rogat; ille favet.

Vir nemus impugnat lassans in caede securim:

Arboris omne genus una ruina trahit.

---

arbor, **arboris** *f.*: a tree
armo (1): to equip
audeo (2) **ausus sum**: to dare
caedes, **caedis** *f.*: murder, slaughter
egeo (2): to lack, be without (+ *abl.*)
faveo (2): to grant a favor
genus, **generis** *n.*: a kind, sort, variety
impugno (1): to fight against, attack
lasso (1): to tire, wear out

lucus, **-i** *m.*: a grove
nemus, **nemoris** *n.*: wood, forest
rogo (1): to ask, ask for
ruina, **-ae** *f.*: fall, catastrophe, destruction
seco (1): to cut
securis, **securis** *f.*: an ax
teneo (2): to hold, support
traho (3): to draw, drag, haul
vir, **viri** *m.*: a man

---

quo teneatur: pres. subj. in rel. clause of characteristic, "lacks (something) *by which it is held*" i.e. a handle

ausa: perf. part., "an ax *having dared* to cut nothing" i.e. able to cut nothing

secare securis: *figura etymologica*

armet: pres. subj. in ind. quest. after *rogat*, "the man asks the grove *to equip her* (the ax)

ille: i.e. the grove

Lucus ait: "Pereo. Mihimet sum causa pericli,

    Me necat ex dono rustica dextra meo."

Unde perire queas, hostem munire caveto:

    Qui dat quo pereat, quem juvat hoste perit.

---

causa, **-ae** *f.*: a cause, source
caveo (2): to beware, avoid
dextra, **-ae** *f.*: a right hand
donum, **-i** *n.*: a gift, present
hostis, **-is** *m/f.*: an enemy
juvo (1): to help, assist

munio (4): to fortify, strengthen
neco (1): to kill, murder
pereo (4): to die, pass away
periclum, **-i** *n.*: danger, peril
queo (3): to be able to (+ *inf.*)
rusticus, **-a**, **-um**: country, rustic

---

mihimet: *-met* is intensive, "cause *to my own self*"
queas: pres. subj. in relative clause of characteristic, "whence *you could* die"
caveto: fut. imper., "beware" + inf.
quo pereat: pres. subj. in rel. clause of characteristic, "by which he may perish"
hoste: abl. of cause, "dies *from an enemy* whom he helps"

Fable 54: De cane et lupo

Another popular fable, "The Dog and the Wolf" seems to have been particularly important to medieval readers, as the last nine lines are marked with paragraph indicators in a number of manuscript copies. The theme in this fable remains popular today. A wolf befriends a dog, and the dog begins to tell of all the luxuries that his master provides, including a warm bed and an abundance of food. The wolf is almost convinced to join the dog in this lifestyle until he notes the bare patches on the dog's neck. The dog explains that those are left by the chains which bind him during the day so that he doesn't injure anyone. The wolf explains that he would rather be a beggar and remain free than be fettered. Much like the country mouse and the ant of earlier fables, the wolf chooses to remain poor and retain his freedom, and the moral praises this.

Cum cane silva lupum sociat. Lupus inquit: "Amoena
    Pelle nites, in te copia sancta patet."
Pro verbis dat verba canis: "Me ditat erilis
    Gratia, cum domino me cibat ipsa domus.
Nocte vigil fures latratu nuntio, tutam
    Servo domum; mihi dat culmus in aede torum."

---

aedis, -is *f.*: a dwelling
amoenus, -a, -um: beautiful, attractive
canis, canis *m/f.*: a dog, hound
cibo (1): to feed, give food
copia, -ae *f.*: plenty, abundance
culmus, -i *m.*: hay, straw
dito (1): to enrich
dominus, -i *m.*: a lord, master
domus, -i *f.*: a house, household
erilis, erile: of a master or mistress
fur, furis *m./f.*: a thief, robber
gratia, -ae *f.*: goodwill, kindness
inquit: he says
latratus, -us *m.*: barking

lupus, -i *m.*: a wolf
niteo (2): to shine, glitter
nox, noctis *f.*: night
nuntio (1): to announce, report
pateo (2): to be well known, be accessible
pellis, pellis *f.*: skin, hide
sanctus, -a, -um: holy, inviolable
servo (1): to watch over, protect
silva, -ae *f.*: wood, forest
socio (1): to unite, join
torus, -i *m.*: a bed, cushion
tutus, -a, -um: safe, secure
verbum, -i *n.*: a word, proverb
vigil, vigilis (*gen.*): awake, wakeful

cum cane: abl. of accompaniment, "joins *with a dog*"
pelle: abl. of specification, "you shine *in your* beautiful *skin*"
nocte: abl. of time when, "awake *at night*"
tutam: perd. acc., "I keep the house *safe*"

Haec movet ore lupus: "Cupio me vivere tecum:

Communem capiant otia nostra cibum."

Reddit verba canis: "Cupio te vivere mecum;

Una dabit nobis mensa manusque cibum."

Ille favet sequiturque canem gutturque caninum

Respicit et querit: "Cur cecidere pili?";

Inquit: "Ne valeam morsu peccare diurno,

Vincla diurna fero, nocte labante vagor."

Reddit verba lupus: "Non est mihi copia tanti

Ut fieri servus ventris amore velim.

---

amor, amoris *m.*: love, affection
cado (3) **cecidi**: fall
caninus, -a, -um: of a dog
capio (3): to take hold, seize
cibus, -i *m.*: food
communis, commune: common, shared
diurnus, -a, -um: by day
faveo (2): to befriend, support
fero, ferre: to receive, get
fio, fieri: to be made
guttur, gutturis: throat, neck
labor (1): to glide
manus, manus *f.*: a hand
mensa, -ae *f.*: a table
morsus, morsus *m.*: a bite
moveo (2): to move, stir
noster, -a, -um: our

os, oris *n.*: a mouth, speech
otium, -i *n.*: leisure, spare time
pecco (1): to sin, do wrong
pilus, -i *m.*: hair
quaero (3): to ask, inquire
reddo (3): to return
respicio (3): to look back at, consider
sequor (3): to follow
servus, -i *m.*: a slave, servant
tantus, -a, -um: so great, so much
unus, -a, -um: one
vagor (1): to wander, roam
valeo (2): to be strong, prevail
venter, ventris *m.*: a stomach
vinclum, -i *n.*: a chain, bond
vivo (3): to live, reside
volo, velle: wish, want

---

ore: abl. of means, "moved these things *with his mouth*" i.e. he speaks
capiant: pres. subj. jussive, "*let* our leisure *seize* food" i.e. let us seize food at out leisure
una mensa manusque: nom., "*one hand and one table* will give"
cecidere (=ceciderunt): perf., "why *have* your hairs *fallen out?*"
ne valeam: pres. subj. in purpose clause, "*lest I be able* to sin"
morsu: abl. of manner, "to sin *by biting*"
nocte labente: abl. abs., "I wander with *the night gliding by*" i.e. at night
ut ... velim: pres. subj. in result clause, "so great *so that I wish* to become"
amore: abl. of cause, "*because of the love* of the stomach"

Ditior est liber mendicus divite servo:

    Servus habet nec se nec sua, liber habet;

Libertas, praedulce bonum, bona cetera condit:

    Qua nisi conditur, nil sapit esca mihi.

Libertas animi cibus est et vera voluptas,

    Qua qui dives erit, ditior esse nequit.

Nolo velle meum pro turpi vendere lucro;

    Has qui vendit opes, hic agit ut sit inops."

Non bene pro toto libertas venditur auro:

    Hoc celeste bonum praeterit orbis opes.

---

ago (3): to drive, act
animus, -i *m.*: mind, soul
aurum, -i *n.*: gold
bonum, -i *n.*: good
celestis, celeste: heavenly
ceterus, -a, -um: the remaining, rest
condo (3): to put together, preserve
ditior, -us: rich, wealthy
dives, divitis (*gen.*): rich, wealthy
esca, -ae *f.*: food, meat
inops, inopis (*gen.*): weak, poor
liber, -a, -um: free
libertas, libertatis *f.*: freedom, liberty
lucrum, -i *n.*: gain, profit, avarice
mendicus, -i *m.*: a beggar

nequeo, nequire: be unable (+ *inf.*)
nolo, nolle: to be unwilling, wish not to
ops, opis *f.*: power, might
orbis, orbis *m.*: the orb, world
praedulcis, praedulce: very sweet
praetereo, praeterire: surpass, excel
sapio (3): to be tasty
servus, servi *m.*: a slave, servant
totus, -a, -um: whole, all
turpis, -e: disgraceful, shameful
vendo (3): to sell
verus, -a, -um: true, real
volo, velle: wish, want, be willing
voluptas, voluptatis *f.*: pleasure, delight

---

divite servo: abl. of comparison, "wealthier *than a rich slave*"
qua: abl. of specficiation with *dives* with antecedent *libertas*, "rich *in which thing*"
velle: pres. inf. object of *vendere*, "to sell my *willing*" i.e. my free will
pro turpi lucro: "sell *for vile gain*"
ut sit: pres. subj. in purpose clause, "acts *so that he is* poor"

Fable 55: De ventre et membris

This fable seems to reflect the Biblical idea of each member of the church body contributing an equal amount, found in 1 *Corinthians* 12:12-22, with which the medieval reader certainly could have been familiar. The scripture invokes a scenario in which one part of the body decides that it does not want to serve the rest of the body, and compares this to the members of the church working together. This fable elaborates this idea; the foot and the hand complain about the easy life that the stomach lives: it receives the profits of the work that the rest of the body preforms, but doesn't have to do any work itself. The hand and foot suddenly refuse to feed the stomach, but, of course, this leads to the death of the body. The moral corresponds to the Biblical idea that no man can subsist alone.

> Incusant avidi pes et manus otia ventris:
>
> "Omnia solus habes lucra, labore cares.
>
> Nos labor edomuit, te fovit inertia: sorbes
>
> Omnia, quae nostri cura laboris emit.
>
> Disce pati famis acre jugum vel disce labori
>
> Cedere, teque tui cura laboris alat."

---

acer, acris: sharp, bitter
alo (3): to feed, nourish
avidus, -a, -um: greedy
careo (2): to be without, lack
cedo (3): to concede, yield
cura, -ae *f.*: care, pains
disco (3): to learn to (+ *inf.*)
edomo (1) **edomui**: conquer, overcome
emo (3): to gain, acquire
fames, famis *f.*: hunger, want
foveo (2): to keep warm, favor
incuso (1): to criticize, condemn

inertia, -ae *f.*: ignorance, inactivity
jugum, -i *n.*: a yoke
labor, laboris *m.*: labor, work
lucrum, -i *n.*: gain, profit
membrum, -i *n.*: a member, limb
otium, -i *n.*: leisure
patior (3): to suffer, endure
pes, pedis *m.*: a foot
solus, -a, -um: only, alone
sorbeo (2): to drink, absorb
venter, -tris *n.*: a stomach

---

labore: abl. of sep., "you lack *labor*" i.e. you jdon't work
famis acre jugum: "the fierce yoke of hunger"
labori: adt. after cedere, "yield *to labor*" i.e. agree to work
alat: pres. subj. jussive, "and *let* the pain of your labor *feed* you"

Sic ventri servire negant; se venter inanem

    Comperit, orat opem: nil dat avara manus.

Ille preces iterat: iterum fugit illa precantem.

    In stomachi fundo torpet obitque calor;

Victa fame natura fugit, vis arida fauces

    Obserat ut solitum non sinat ire cibum.

Vult epulas dare sera manus, sed corporis aegri

    Perdita non reparans machina tota perit.

Nemo sibi satis est: eget omnis amicus amico.

    Si non vis alii parcere, parce tibi.

---

aeger, -a, -um: sick, ill
amicus, -i *m.*: a friend
aridus, -a, -um: dried, thirsty
avarus, -a -um: avaricious, greedy
calor, caloris *m.*: heat, warmth
comperio (4): to learn, discover
corpus, corporis *n.*: a body
egeo (2): to need (+ *abl.*)
eo, ire: to go
epula, -ae *f.*: food
fames, famis *f.*: hunger, famine
faux, faucis *f.*: a throat
fugio (3): to flee, fly
fundus, -i *m.*: bottom, lowest part
inanis, inane: void, empty
itero (1): to do a second time, repeat
iterum: again
machina, -ae *f.*: a machine
natura, -ae *f.*: nature
nego (1): to deny, refuse (+ *inf.*)

nemo, neminis *m./f.*: no one, nobody
obeo, obire: to die
obsero (1): to fasten, shut off
ops, opis *f.*: wealth
oro (1): to beg, ask for
parco (3): to spare, show consideration
perdo (3) **perdidi, perditus**: to ruin, destroy
pereo (4): to die, pass away
precor (1): to beg, implore
prex, precis *f.*: a prayer, request
reparo (1): to renew, revive
satis: enough, adequately
serus, -a, -um: too late
servio (4): to serve (+ *dat.*)
sino (3): to allow, permit
solitus, -a, -um: usual, customary
stomachus, -i *m.*: a gullet, stomach
torpeo (2): to be numb or lethargic
vinco (3) **vici, victus**: to conquer, defeat
vis, viris *f.*: strength, power

---

inanem: acc. pred., "discovered itself to be *empty*"
ille ... illa: "the stomach ... the hand"
victa: perf. part. nom., "*having been overcome* by hunger, substance flees"
ut...sinat: pres subj. in result clause, "*so that it does not permit*" + inf.
sera: nom. agreeing with *manus*, "the hand *too late* wishes"
alii: dat. after *parcere*, "to be sparing *to another*"

Fable 56: De simia et vulpe

An ape is upset about her ugly child and tries to convince a vixen to give part of her tail to the child so that it might be more beautiful. The ape's logic argues that the vixen's tail is just a useless weight to her anyway and she can certainly spare part of it. The vixen replies that she is happy with her tail, which she considers to be light and short. The moral notes that something which a greedy person might try to downplay can be important to a poor man.

Simia de turpi queritur nate; porrigit aures

Vulpes: non recipit mente, sed aure preces.

Simia sic fatur: "Natis ut mihi dedecus ornem

Sufficeret caudae pars mihi parva tuae.

Quid prodest nimia campos insculpere cauda

Quod mihi prodesset, est tibi pondus iners."

Illa refert: "Nimio damnas de pondere caudam:

Est brevis estque levis; haec duo damna queror.

---

auris, auris *f.*: an ear
brevis, breve: short, little
campus, -i *m.*: a plane, level field
cauda, -ae *f.*: a tail
damno (1): to condemn
damnum, -i *n.*: damage
dedecus, dedecoris *n.*: disgrace
duo, duae, duo: two
iners, inertis (*gen.*): helpless
insculpo (3): to carve, scrape
levis, leve: light, thin
natis, -is *f.*: buttocks
nimius, -a, -um: excessive, too great

orno (1): to furnish, decorate
pars, partis *f.*: a part, share
parvus, -a, -um: small, little
pondus, ponderis *n.*: a weight, burden
porrigo (3): to stretch out, extend
prosum, prodesse: be useful
queror (3): to complain, protest
recipio (3): to accept, take in
refero, referre: recall, reply
simia, -ae *m./f.*: a monkey, ape
sufficio (3): to be sufficient, suffice
vulpes, vulpis *f.*: a fox

---

mente...aure: abl. of means, "does not accept *in her mind* but *in her ear*"
natis deducus: "the disgrace of my buttocks" the plural (*natium*) is more normal for this meaning
ut ornem: pres. subj. in result clause after sufficeret, "could suffice *for me to decorate*"
sufficeret: impf. subj. potential, "a small part *could suffice*"
nimia cauda: abl. of means, " to carve the plain *with too great a tail*" i.e. by dragging it on the ground
quod mihi prodesset: impf. subj. potential, "which could be a proft to me"

Malo verrat humum quam sit tibi causa decoris,

　　Quam tegat immundas res bene munda nates."

Id nimium minimoque minus ditaret egenum,

　　Quod nimium minimo credis, avare, minus.

avarus, -i: greedy person	**malo, malle**: to prefer
causa, -ae *f.*: a cause, reason	**minor, minus**: less
credo (3): to believe	**mundus, -a, -um**: clean
decus, decoris *n.*: glory, honor	**natis, natis** *f.*: a rump
dito (1): to enrich	**nimium, -i** *n.*: excess
egenus, -i *m.*: a poor man	**nimium**: (*adv.*) very
humus, -i *f.*: ground, soil	**tego** (3): to cover, hide
immundus, -a, -um: dirty, filthy	**verro** (3): to swee

verrat: pres. subj. in noun clause after *malo*, I prefer *that it sweep*"

quam sit ... quam teget: pres. subj. in noun clause of comparison after *malo*, "*than that it be ... than that* a clean thing *cover*"

id nimium ... avare, minus: these two lines are highly mannered. The following reordering of the words suggests one rendering: *id nimium minimoque minus, quod credis, avare, (esse) minus nimium minimo, ditaret egenum*, "that excess and by the least less, which you, avaricious one, believe (to be) less than the very least, could enrich a needy person"

id nimium minimoque minus: "that excess and (amount) less than the least" a paradoxical statement. The ape claims that the piece of tail is both an excess (*nimium*) to the fox and also a very small thing.

ditaret: impf. subj. potential, "that thing *could enrich*"

avare: voc., "Oh greedy one"

Fable 57: De institore et asino

The moral of this fable endorses seeking revenge; an ass wishes for death because he is treated so cruelly by his master. The fable, however, notes that pain might live on beyond death, because the ass's hide might be used to make small drums, and therefore he will continue to be beaten. The moral then states that man cannot find rest in death, but instead in seeking revenge-- a very non-Biblical lesson.

Dum fora festinus lucro petit, instat asello

Institor et pressum pondere fuste premit.

Ille necem sperat, nece promittente quietem,

Sed nece completa, vivere poena potest:

---

asellus, -i *m.*: a small ass, donkey
asinus, -i *m.*: an ass, donkey
compleo (2): to fill up, complete
festinus, -a, -um: swift, quick
forum, -i *n.*: a market
fustis, fustis *m.*: a staff, club, stick
institor, institoris *m.*: a shopkeeper
insto (1): to pursue, threaten (+ *dat.*)
lucrum, -i *n.*: profit

nex, necis *f.*: death
peto (3): to reach towards, make for
poena, -ae *f.*: a penalty, punishment
pondus, ponderis *n.*: a weight, burden
premo (3) **pressi, pressus**: to press, strike
promitto (3): to promise
quies, quietis *f.*: rest, peace
spero (1): to hope for
vivo (3): to be alive, live

---

festinus: nom., "he seeks *in haste*"
lucro: dative of purpose, "seeks the market *for a profit*"
pressus ... premit: "*he pressed* him *pressed* by his burden"
fuste: abl. of means, "strikes him *with a stick*"
nece promittente: abl. abs., "death promising"
nece completa: abl. abs., "but death having been complete"

Nam cribella facit et tympana pellis aselli,

    Haec lassatur et haec pulsa tonante manu.

Cui sua vita nocet, caveat sibi rumpere vitam.

    Non nece, sed meriti jure quiescit homo.

caveo (2): to beware
cribellum, -i *n.*: a small sieve
homo, hominis *m.*: a man
jus, juris *n.*: justice
lasso (1): to tire, weary
meritum, meriti *n.*: merit, service
noceo (2): to harm, hurt

pellis, pellis *f.*: skin, hide
pello (3) **pepuli, pulsus**: beat, drive out
quiesco (3): to find rest
rumpo (3): to break, destroy
tono (1): to thunder
tympanum, -i *n.*: a small drum
vita, -ae *f.*: life

tonante manu: abl. means, "struck *with a thundering hand*

haec ... haec: nom. subj., "*this* is struck and *that*" i.e. the skin as sieve and drum, respectively

sua vita: nom., "whose *own life* harms"

caveat: pres. subj. jussive, "*let him beware* to break life i.e. commit suicide

meriti jure: abl., "finds quiet *from justice of service*" i.e. by just service

Fable 58: De cervo

The last three fables in the elegiac Romulus read much more like animal tales than the rest of the collection; even their moral lessons seem a bit forced, and it has been speculated that whoever the compiler and translator of the elegiac Romulus is must have added these three fables. In this first story, a stag is fleeing a hunter and finds himself in a barn. He convinces an ox to help him hide himself, and the ox is able to bury him in enough hay that he escapes the eye of the plowman. After this incident, the ox cautions that while the disguise worked one time, it will not work on the next stable hand-- who is so vigilant that the oxen compares him to Argus, the mythical giant with hundreds of eyes. Indeed, although the stag reburies himself, the next man easily spots him when he gives the oxen extra fodder, and rejoices that now he has found food for himself as well. The moral however only speaks of how the outcome of this fable is true to nature; a man living in exile is not his own and a powerful man is watchful; and for good measure the fable also adds that servants often snore and good men want help.

Motus voce canum cervus fugit, avia silvae

   Deserit, arva tenet, claustra bovina subit.

Bos ait: "Aut luci tenebras aut aequora campi

   Tutius intrares, hinc piger, inde levis.

Huc veniet custosque boum stabulique magister:

---

aequor, aequoris *n.*: level plain	**levis, -e:** light
arvum, -i *n.*: cultivated land	**lucus, luci** *m.*: dark wood
avium, -i *n.*: a pathless region, lonely places	**magister, -i** *m.*: a master
bos, bovis *m./f.*: an ox, bull	**moveo** (2) **movi, motus**: to move, provoke
bovinus, -a, -um: of cattle/oxen/cows	**piger, -a, -um:** slow
campus, -i *m.*: a plane, level field	**silva, -ae** *f.*: wood, forest
canis, canis *n.*: a dog, hound	**stabulum, -i** *n.*: a stall, stable, herd
cervus, -i *m.*: a stag, deer	**subeo** (4): go into, approach
claustrum, -i *n.*: an enclosure	**tenebra, -ae** *f.*: darkness
custos, custodis *m./f.*: a guard	**teneo** (2): to hold, keep
desero (3): to leave, depart	**tutus, -a, -um:** safe, secure
fugio (3): to flee, fly	**vox, vocis** *f.*: a voice, tone

---

voce: abl. of means, "having been provoked *by the barking*"

intrares: imperf. subj. potential, "*you could enter* more safely"

custosque boum stabulique: polysyndeton

vel tantum ... alter: "both *or even one*"

Si duo vel tantum te videt alter, obis."

Cervus ait: "Mihi vestra necem clementia demat:

   Condite me latebris, dum juvet umbra fugam."

Hunc tumulat faenum. Praesepe revisit arator:

   Frondibus et faeno munit alitque boves.

Hic redit ac cervus vitasse pericula gaudet,

   Bobus agit grates. E quibus unus ait:

"Est leve vitare caecum. Si venerit Argus,

   Argum si poteris fallere, victor eris.

---

ago (3): to thank (+ *gratias*)
alo (3): to feed, nourish
alter, -a, -um: one (of two)
arator, aratoris *m.*: a plowman, farmer
Argus, -i *m.*: Argus, mythical watchmen
caecus, -i *m.*: a blind person
clementia, -ae *f.*: mercy, clemency
condo (3): to conceal, hide
demo (3): to take away
faenum, -i *n.*: hay
fallo (3): to deceive
frons, frondis *f.*: foliage, leaves
fuga, -ae *f.*: a flight, fleeing
gaudeo (2): to be glad, rejoice
grates, gratis *f.*: thanks

juvo (1): to help, assist
latebra, -ae *f.*: a hiding place, retreat
munio (4): to fortify, strengthen
obeo, obire: to fall, die
periculum, -i *n.*: danger, peril
praesepe, -is *n.*: a manger
redeo, redire: to return, go back
reviso (3): to revisit, go back and see
tumulo (1): to bury
umbro (1): to cast a shadow on
unus, -a, -um: one
vester, -a, -um: your
victor, victoris *m.*: a conqueror, victor
video (2): to see, look at
vito (1): to avoid, evade

---

demat: pres. subj. jussive, "*let* your mercy *take away!*"

latebris: abl. of place where, "conceal me *in a hiding place*"

dum juvet: pres. subj. in general temporal clause, "until the shade helps flight" (whenever that may be)

frondibus et faeno: abl. of means, "fortifies and feeds *with foliage and hay*"

vitasse: perf. inf. (=vitavisse) complementing gaudet, "he rejoices *to have avoided*"

bobus: dat, "gave thanks *to the oxen*"

vitare: pres. inf. epexegetic after *leve*, "easy *to avoid*"

si venerit: fut. perf. in fut. more vivid protasis, "if Argus shall come" Argus had 100 eyes and was sent by Hera to watch over Io

Centum fert oculos; cui se debere fatentur

Et domus et servi totaque jura loci.

Res tua te reperit Argum, res altera caecum.

Qui tibi dormitat scit vigilare sibi."

Hic silet. Argus init stabulum bobusque ministrat;

Plus aequo tenues viderat esse boves.

Dum munit presepe cibo, dum fulgurat ira,

Ausa videre diem cornua longa videt.

---

aequus, -a, -um: equal, reasonable
audeo (2) **ausus sum**: to dare to (+ *inf.*)
caecus, -a, -um: blind
centum: 100
cibus, -i *m.*: food
cornu, cornus *n.*: a horn
debeo (2): to owe
dies, diei *m./f.*: day, daylight
domus, -i *f.*: a house, household
dormito (1): to feel sleepy, drowsy
fateor (2): to admit, confess
fero, ferre: to bring, bear
fulguro (1): to flash, shine brightly
ineo, inire: to enter, go in
ira, -ae *f.*: anger, ire

locus, -i *m.*: a neighborhood, region
longus, -a, -um: long, tall
ministro (1): to attend (to), serve
munio (4): to fortify
oculus, -i *m.*: an eye
plus: (*adv.*) more
reperio (4): to discover, obtain, light on
scio (3): to know, understand
servus, -i *m.*: a slave, servant
sileo (2): to be silent
stabulum, -i *n.*: a stall, stable
tenuis, tenue: thin, fine
totus, -a, -um: whole, all
vigilo (1): to remain awake

---

fatentur: personal use of ind. st., "to whom *they are said* to owe"

tota jura: nom. pl., "*all the authorities* of the place"

Argum ... caecum: acc. pred., "finds you *an Argus ... blind*"

tenues: acc. pred., "to be more *thin*"

aequo: abl. of comparision, "to be much thinner *than reasonable*" i.e. than normal

ausa: perf. part. acc. agreeing with *cornua*, "he sees antlers *which have dared* to see the daylight" i.e. the stag has stuck his head out of the woods to see

cornua longa: acc. pl., "long horns," i.e. antlers

"Quid latet hic? Quid" ait "Video?" Sentitque latentem

Et bona fortunae munera laetus habet.

Exulis est non esse suum, vigilare potentis,

Stertere servorum, velle juvare pii.

bonus, -a, -um: good
exul, exulis *m./f.*: exile
fortuna, -ae *f.*: fate
habeo (2): to have, hold
laetus, -a, -um: happy
lateo (2): to lie hidden, lurk
munus, muneris *n.*: a gift

pius, a, -um: upright, faithful
potens, potentis (*gen.*): powerful, strong
sentio (4): to perceive
sterto (3): to snore
vigilo (1): to remain awake, watch
volo, velle: to wish, want

esse ... vigilare ... stertere ... juvare: all infinitives used as subjects of *est*: "Not *to be* his own is ... *to watch* is ... etc"

exulis ... potentis ... servorum ... pii: gen. pred., "is *the exile's* ... is *the powerful man's* ... etc." i.e. is characteristic of the exile ... of the powerful man ... etc.

Fable 59: De Judaeo et pincerna

There is no clear reason to cast the Jew in this fable, other than that he is a wealthy man, and this ethnic casting seems to fit medieval stereotypes. The wealthy Jew works to endear himself to the king by giving gifts, and asks to be guided to the king by the king's butler. On the journey, however, the butler is overcome with greed and decides to kill the Jew. The Jew protests, noting that the partridge sitting in the nearby tree will tell of the deed, but the butler scoffs and kills him anyway. A year passes and the butler is serving partridge to the king, and after eating he begins to laugh uncontrollably. The king questions this, and eventually the butler spills the story of the Jew's murder. The king is upset, and orders the butler crucified. The moral to this fable is related, but generic, warning that gold should not persuade you to slay anyone.

Fert Judaeus opes, sed onus fert pectore majus:

Intus adurit eum cura laborque foris.

Ergo, metu damni, sibi munere regis amorem

Firmat, ut accepto produce tutus eat.

Regius hunc pincerna regit, cor cuius adurit

Auri dira sitis, qui parat ense nefas.

---

accipio (3) **accepi, acceptus**: to take, receive
aduro (3): to scorch, burn
amor, amoris *m.*: love, affection
aurum, -i *n.*: gold
cor, cordis *n.*: heart, mind
cura, -ae *f.*: concern, worry
damnum, -i *n.*: loss
dirus, -a -um: awful, dire
ensis, ensis *m.*: a sword
fero, ferre: to bring, bear
firmo (1): to strengthen, harden
foris: on the outside
intus: within, on the inside
Judaeus, -i *m.*: a Jew

labor, laboris *m.*: labor
major, majus: larger, greater
metus, metus *m.*: fear, anxiety
nefas (*indecl.*): sin
onus, oneris *n.*: a load, burden
ops, opis *f.*: wealth
paro (1): to prepare
pectus, pectoris *n.*: breast, heart
pincerna, -ae *m.*: a cupbearer, butler
produx, -ducis *m.*: a guide
regius, -a, -um: royal, of a king
rego (3): to rule, guide
rex, regis *m.*: a king
sitis, sitis *f.*: a thirst for (+ *gen.*)

---

pectore: abl. of place where, "carries *in his heart*"
metu: abl. of cause, "*because of fear* he strengthens"
munere: abl. of means, "strengthens *with service*"
ut eat: pres. subj. purpose clause, "*in order to go* safely"

Silva patet, subeunt. Judaeus in ore sequentis
    Cor notat: "Ipse sequar," inquit; at ille negat
Et gladium nudans: "Nemo sciet," inquit "Obito."
    Ille refert: "Scelus hoc ista loquetur avis."
Prosilit a dumo perdix: hanc indice signat.
    Alter ait: "Scelus hoc ista loquetur avis?"
Et rapit ense caput et opes metit et scrobe funus
    Celat. Agit celeres annus in orbe rotas.
Perdices domini cenae pincerna ministrat,
    Ridet et a risu vix vacat ille suo.

---

ago (3): to drive
annus, -i *m.*: a year
avis, avis *f.*: a bird
caput, capitis *n.*: a head
celer, celeris, -e: swift, quick
celo (1): to conceal, hide
cena, -ae *f.*: dinner, meal
dominus, -i *m.*: a lord, master
dumus, -i *m.*: a briar bush
funus, funeris *n.*: a burial, corpse
gladius, -i *m.*: a sword
index, indicis *m.*: a hand
loquor (3): to speak, report
meto (3): to mow, reap
ministro (1): to attend (to), serve
nego (1): to deny
noto (1): to observe, record
nudo (1): to lay bare, strip
obeo, obire: to die

orbis, orbis *m.*: a circle
os, oris *n.*: a mouth, face
pateo (2): to stand open, be open
perdix, perdicis *m./f.*: a partridge
prosilio (4): to jump, leap up
rapio (3): to seize, carry off
refero, referre: to repeat, recall
rideo (2): to laugh, ridicule
risus, risus *m.*: laughter
rota, -ae *f.*: a wheel
scelus, sceleris *n.*: a crime, calamity
scio (4): to know, understand
scrobis, scrobis *m./f.*: a ditch, trench
sequor (3): to follow
signo (1): to mark, designate
silva, -ae *f.*: wood, forest
vaco (1): to be vacant, abstain from
vix: hardly, scarcely

---

accepto produce: "a guide having been received" i.e. from the king
sequentis: pres. part., "on the face *of the one following*"
obito: fut. imper. of *obeo*, "die!"
hanc: the partridge
indice: abl. of means, "designates *with his hand*" i.e. points to
scrobe: abl. of place where, "hides *in a ditch*"
rotas: "drives the swift *wheels*" i.e. the "rotations" of the seasons but also the "wheels" of the sun's chariot
cenae: dat. of purpose, "serves *for the dinner* of the master"
ille: the butler

138

Rex audire sitit; hic differet dicere causam.

Fit locus, ambo sedent: hic petit, ille refert.

Rex dolet et laeto mentitur gaudia vultu.

Regis concilium consiliumque sedet:

Pincernam crucis esse reum sententia prodit:

Crux punit meritum jure favente cruci.

Ut perimas quemquam nullum tibi suadeat aurum:

Nam decus et vitam maesta ruina rapit.

---

ambo, -ae, -o: both
audio (4): to hear
aurum, i *n.*: gold
causa, -ae *f.*: a cause
concilium, -i *n.*: a council
consilium, -i *n.*: counsel, deliberation
decus, decoris *n.*: honor, glory
dico (3): to say, talk
differo, differre: to postpone, delay (+ *inf.*)
doleo (2): to hurt, grief
faveo (2): to favor (+ *dat.*)
fio, fiere: to become, happen
gaudium, -i *n.*: joy
jus, juris *n.*: justice
laetus, -a, -um: happy, glad
locus, -i *m.*: a place, opportunity

maestus, -a, -um: sad
mentior (4): to lie, pretend
meritus, -a, -um: deserving
perimo (3): to kill, destroy
peto (3): to seek
prodeo (4): to go out, advance
punio (4): to punish
refero, referre: to recount recall
reus, -a, -um: guilty
ruina, -ae *f.*: fall
sedeo (2): to sit
sententia, -ae *f.*: an opinion
sitio (4): to be thirsty, desire to (+ *inf.*)
suadeo (2): to urge, suggest
vultus, vultus *m.*: a face

---

laeto ... vultu: abl. of means, "pretends *with a glad expression*"
concilium consiliumque: an example of *zeugma*, since the verb is strictly appropriate only to the first of these nouns, which are often exchanged for one another, "the counsel sits and deliberates"
crucis: gen. after *reum*, "guilty of a cross," i.e. guilty of a crime worthy of crucifixion
prodit: introducing ind. st., "*advances* that the butler is"
jure favente: abl. abs., "*with justice favoring* the cross"
ut perimas: pres. subj. in noun clause after *suadeat*, "persuade you *to kill*"
suadeat: pres. subj. jussive, "*let* no gold *persuade*!"

Fable 60: De cive et equite

This tale is by far the longest of all the fables, and the narrative is significantly more complicated than any other. Two men serve a king, an old man and a knight. The knight grows jealous of the old man and accuses him of theft. He attempts to prove this by challenging him to a fight, hoping to kill him and gain the sole attention of the king. The old man gets his plowman to fight for him, and when the battle begins, the plowman acts as though he is weak for quite some time. Eventually, he shows his true strength, and hits the knight on the crown of his head. This brings the knight to the ground, and he is unable to get up. The plowman is declared victor by refusing to strike the knight until he rises, and forcing the knight to admit that he is not physically capable of rising. The moral, again, is rather vague, first it notes that justice overcomes power, which fits with the fable, but then goes on to say that love offers more than hatred, and trust more than treachery, both lessons which are less clear from the tale.

Civis, eques sub rege vigent: hic proelia regis,

    Hic dispensat opes; hic vir et ille senex.

Invidiae, perflata genis, innata doloris

    Flammis, fax juvenem torret honore senis.

Regis in aure truces figit de cive susurros:

    "Est tibi non pastor, sed lupus ille senex.

---

auris, auris *f.*: an ear
civis, civis *m./f.*: a citizen, commoner
dispenso (1): to manage, distribute
dolor, doloris *m.*: pain, anguish
eques, equitis *m.*: a horseman, knight
fax, facis *f.*: a torch, fire
figo (3): to fasten, fix
flamma, -ae *f.*: flame
gena, -ae *f.*: cheeks
honor, honoris *m.*: honor, respect
innascor, innasci, innatus sum (3): to be born
invidia, -ae *f.*: envy

juvenis, juvenis *m./f.*: a youth, young man
ops, opis *f.*: wealth
pastor, pastoris *m.*: a shepherd, herdsman
perflo (1): to blow through
proelium, -i *n.*: a battle
rex, regis *m.*: a king
senex, senis *m.*: an old man
susurrus, -i *m.*: a whisper
torreo (2): to parch, roast
trux, trucis (*gen.*): wild, savage
vigeo (2): to thrive, flourish
vir, -i *m.*: a man

---

invidiae: gen. with *fax*, "the fire *of envy*"
perflata ... innata: perf. part., "*having been incited ... having been born* from the flames of grief
honore: abl. of cause, "burns *because of honor*"

Ditant furta senem, crevit sua copia furtis,

  Est sua de censu gaza recisa tuo.

Firmabo mea verba manu, sua furta fateri

  Hunc faciam: bello judice, verus ero."

Cum moveant objecta senem, plus debilis aetas

  Hunc movet ac senii crimine visus hebes.

Parcunt jura seni si pro sene pugnet amicus,

  Cui nullius odor faenoris arma probat.

Mendicat pugilem, sed abest qui pugnet amicus:

  Nam refugit, viso turbine, falsus amor;

---

absum, abesse: be away, absent
aetas, aetatis *f.*: lifetime, age
amicus, -i *m.*: a friend
amor, amoris *m.*: love, affection
armum, -i *n.*: arms
bellum, -i *n.*: a war, battle
census, census *m.*: wealth, property
copia, -ae *f.*: plenty, wealth
cresco (3) crevi: to thrive, increase
crimen, criminis *n.*: a crime, fault
debilis, debile: weak, feeble
dito (1): to enrich
faenus, fenoris *n.*: interest, profit, gain
falsus, -a, -um: false, deceiving, feigned
fateor (2): to admit, confess (+ *acc.*)
firmo (1): to support, prove
furtum, -i *n.*: theft, trick
gaza, -ae *f.*: treasure
hebes, hebetis (*gen.*): sluggish, weak

judex, judicis *m.*: a judge, juror
manus, manus *f.*: a hand
mendico (1): to beg for
moveo (2): to move, stir, agitate
objectum, -i *n.*: an accusation, charge
odor, odoris *m.*: a hint, inkling, suggestion
parco (3): to show consideration for (+ *dat.*)
plus: (*adv.*) more
probo (1): to demonstrate, prove
pugil, pugilis *m.*: a boxer, champion
pugno (1): to fight
recido (3) recidi, recisus: to cut away
refugio (3): to flee back, run away
senium, -i *n.*: condition of old age
turben, turbinis *n.*: a whirlwind, storm
verbum, -i *n.*: a word
verus, -a, -um: true
visus, -us *m.*: power of sight

---

recisa: perf. part. pred., "his treasure is *cut away*"
manu: abl. of means, "support *by my hand*" i.e. by a physical challenge
fateri: inf. after causative *faciam*, "I will make him *to confess*"
bello judice: abl. abs., "with battle as a judge" i.e. by a trial of strength
cum moveant: pres. subj. in concessive clause, "*although* the accusations *move*"
crimine: abl. of means, "sluggish *by the crime* of old age" ironic
seni: dat. after *parcant*, "shows consideration *to the old man*"
si pugnet: pres. subj. in fut. less vivid protasis, "if a friend were to fight"
cui: dat. of possession, "*whose* arms"
qui pugnet: pres. subj. in rel. clause of characteristics, "a friend *who would fight*"
viso turbine: abl. abs., "with a storm having been seen"

Dum fortuna tonat, fugitivos terret amicos,

    Et quis amet, quis non, sola procella docet.

Cena trahit civem, differt nox una duellum;

    Sollicitat mentem justa querela senis:

"Quos meritis emi, multos mihi fecit amicos

    Longa dies, cunctos abstulit hora brevis.

De tot amicorum populo non restitit unus,

    Quamque dedi multis, nemo repensat opem.

Rebar pace frui: mea paci congruit aetas,

    Sed mea turbavit gaudia livor edax.

---

aetas, aetatis *f.*: lifetime, age
amo (1): to love, like
aufero, auferre, abstuli: to take away, withdraw
brevis, breve,: short, brief, quick
cena, -ae *f.*: dinner, supper
congruo (3): to agree, be suited
cunctus, -a, -um: altogether, all
dies, diei *m./f.*: day
differo, differre: postpone, delay, differ
doceo (2): to teach, show, point out
duellum, -i *n.*: a duel, battle
edax, edacis (*gen.*): greedy, rapacious
emo (3): to buy, gain
fortuna, -ae *f.*: chance, luck, fate
fruor (3): to enjoy, delight in (+ *abl.*)
fugitivus, -a, -um: fugitive, fleeing
gaudium, -i *n.*: joy, delight
hora, -ae *f.*: an hour, time
justus, -a, -um: just, fair

livor, livoris *m.*: envy, spite
meritum, -i *n.*: merit, service
nemo, neminis *m./f.*: no one
nox, noctis *f.*: night
ops, opis *f.*: power, help
pax, pacis *f.*: peace, harmony
populus, -i *m.*: a multitude
procella, -ae *f.*: a storm, gale
querela, -ae *f.*: a complaint
reor (2): to think, suppose
repenso (1): to compensate
resto (1): to stand firm, stay behind, be left
sollicito (1): to disturb, worry
solus, -a, -um: only, alone
terreo (2): to frighten, scare
tono (1): to thunder
tot: so many, many
traho (3): to draw, take
turbo (1): to disturb
unus, -a, -um: one

---

fugitivos amicos: "fair-weather friends"
quis amet: pres. subj. in ind. quest., "teaches *who loves,* who does not"
una duellum: "*one night delays the duel*" a pun on the mean of *duellum* from *duo*
meritis: abl. of means, "whom I bought *with my services*"
longa dies: "a long day" i.e. a long time, by *metonymy*
multis: dat. after *dedi,* "I gave *to many*"
rebar: impf. in personal ind. st., "I was supposing to" + inf. i.e., I was expecting
paci: dat. after congruit, "is suited *to peace*"

Hosti multa meo palmam pepigere: tepesco,

Ille calet; careo viribus, ille viget;

Arma parum novi, se totum praebuit armis.

Est mihi visus hebes, visus acutus ei.

Nil mihi praebet opem nisi justae gratia causae;

De fragili queritur preside causa potens.

Corporis eclipsim timet alti copia cordis:

Nam fragili peccat mens animosa manu.

Si turpes nitide mendax infamia vitae

Infigit maculas, quid nituisse juvat?"

---

acutus, -a, -um :sharp, sharpened
altus, -a, -um, lofty, noble
animosus, -a, -um: bold, noble
caleo (2): to be hot
careo (2): to be without, lack, lose (+ *abl.*)
cor, cordis *n.*: a heart
corpus, corporis *n.*: a body, person
eclipsis, eclipsis *f.*: an eclipse, failure
fragilis, fragile: brittle, frail
gratia, -ae *f.*: favor, kindness
hostis, -is *m/f.*: a enemy
infamia, -ae *f.*: infamy
infigo (3): fasten (on), affix
justus, -a, -um: just, fair
juvo (1): to help, serve
macula, -ae *f.*: a stain, dishonor
mendax, mendacis (*gen.*): false, deceitful
multum, -i *n.*: many things
nil: nothing

nisi: if not, except
niteo (2) **nitui**: shine, look bright
nitidus, -a, -um: shining, bright
nosco (3) **novi**: to get to know, learn
palma, -ae *f.*: a palm award, first place
pango (3) **pepigi**: fix, settle, agree upon
parum: too little, not enough
pecco (1): to stumble, be faulty
potens, potentis (*gen.*): powerful, strong
praebeo (2): to offer
praeses, praesidis *m./f.*: a protector, guard
queror (3): to complain, protest
tepesco (3): to become tepid/lukewarm
timeo (2): to fear, dread
totus, -a, -um: whole, all, total
turpis, -e: ugly, nasty
vigeo (2): to be strong
vis, viris *f.*: strength
vita, -ae *f.*: life

---

hosti meo: dat. after *pepigere*, "fixed first place *for my enemy*"
pepigere: perf. (=*pepigerunt*), "many things *have fixed*"
viribus: abl. of separation after *careo*, "I lack *strength*"
armis: dat. after *praebuit*, "gave himself *to arms*" i.e. devoted himself ot arms
gratia: nom., "nothing offers help except *the favor*"
fragili manu: abl. of manner, "stumbles *with a weak hand*"
nitidae vitae: dat. after compound verb, "has fixed stains *on a shining life*"
nituisse: perf. inf. after iuvat, "what good is it *to have shined*?"

143

Desperat lugetque senex; hunc lenit arator

    Qui senis arva novat, annua lucra ferens:

"Me stimulat pietas pro te perferre duellum,

    Est mihi pro domino dextra parata meo."

Ecce dies oritur, locus est tempusque duello:

    Stant pugiles, inhiant mente manuque sibi.

Est equiti foedum, quod stet, quod pugnet arator,

    Seque putat victum ni cito vincat eum.

Nil de se retinet virtus oblita futuri:

    Dextera corporeas prodiga fundit opes;

---

annuus, -a, -um: yearly, annual
arator, aratoris *m.*: a plowman, farmer
arva, -ae *f.*: arable land, plowed field
cito: quickly, speedily
corporeus, -a, -um: corporeal, bodily
despero (1): to despair
dextera, -ae *f.*: a right hand
dextra, -ae *f.*: a right hand
dominus, -i *m.*: a lord, master
fero, ferre: to bring, bear
foedus, -a, -um: vile, low
fundo (3): to pour, cast
futurus, -a, -um: about to be, future
inhio (1): to gaze eagerly, be eager
lenio (4): to ease, calm
locus, -i *m.*: a place
lucrum, -i *n.*: gain, profit
lugeo (2): to mourn, lament

mens, mentis *f.*: mind
novo (1): to make new, renovate, refresh
oblitus, -a, -um: forgetful (+ *gen.*)
orior (4): to rise, begin
paratus, -a, -um: prepared, ready
perfero, perferre: carry through, perform
pietas, pietatis *f.*: responsibility, loyalty
prodigus, -a, -um: lavish, wasteful
pugil, pugilis *m.*: a boxer, combatant
pugno (1): to fight, dispute
puto (1): to think, believe
retineo (2): to hold back, restrain
stimulo (1): to urge to (+ *inf.*)
sto (1): to stand, stand firm
tempus, temporis *n.*: time
vinco (3) vici, victus: to conquer, defeat
virtus, virtutis *f.*: strength, power

---

mente manuque: abl. of manner, "are eager *with mind and hand*"

quod stet, quod pugnet: pres. subj. in noun clauses that are the subject of *est*, "it is vile *that the farmer would stand, that he would fight*"

victum (*sc.* **esse**): perf. inf. in ind. st., "thinks himself *to have been conquered*"

ni cito vincat: pres. subj. in future less vivid protasis, "if he does not conquer quickly"

nil de se: "holds back *nothing of itself*" i.e. holds nothing in reserve

prodiga: nom. adj. with *dextera*, "the *lavish* right hand pours" i.e pours lavishly

Ictus ipse suos steriles expendit in usus

Et feriens hostem se magis ipse ferit.

Sed propriae virtutis opes abscondit arator

Dum locus expensae detur et hora suae:

Aut motu fallit aut armis temperat ictus

Praedicitque minas frontis utrumque jubar;

Dormitans vigilat et cessans cogitat ictus,

Et metuens audet dextra notatque locum.

Haec mora non artis ratio, sed culpa timoris

Creditur; arte fruens, esse videtur iners.

---

abscondo (3): to hide, conceal
ars, artis *f.*: skill
audeo (2): to be daring
cesso (1): to be inactive, hold back
cogito (1): to contemplate, consider
credo (3): to believe
culpa, -ae *f.*: fault, blame
dormito (1): to feel sleepy, to be sluggish
expendo (3): to pay, pay out, judge
expensa, -ae *f.*: expenditure
fallo (3): to deceive, beguile
ferio (4): to hit, strike
frons, frontis *m./f.*: a forehead, brow
hora, -ae *f.*: hour, time
ictus, ictus *m.*: a blow, stroke
iners, inertis (*gen.*): helpless, unskillful
jubar, jubaris *n.*: radiance, light

locus, -i *m.*: a place, opportunity
magis: more
metuo (3): to fear, be afraid
mina, -ae *f.*:: threat, menace
mora, -ae *f.*: a delay, hindrance
motus, motus *m.*: movement, motion
noto (1): to observe, record
praedico (3): to announce, telegraph
proprius, -a, -um: his own
ratio, rationis *f.*: an account, plan
sterilis, sterile: barren, fruitless
tempero (1): to combine, temper
timor, timoris *m.*: fear, dread
usus, usus *m.*: use
vigilo (1): to remain awake, be vigilant
virtus, virtutis *f.*: strength, power

---

steriles ... in usus: "expends in futile uses" i.e. to no purpose

dum ... detur: pres. subj. implying purpose, "until the place and hour *are given*"

expensae ... suae: gen., "of his own disbursement" i.e. of his own counter blow

motu: abl. of means, "deceives *with his motion*"

utrumque jubar: nom. subject, "*each light* of his brow (i.e. each eye) anounces"

dormitans ... cessans ... metuens: pres. part. concessive, "although sleeping ... yielding ...fearing"

ratio ... culpa: nom. pred. after creditur, "believed to be not *the plan*, but *the fault*"

fruens: pres. part. concessive, "*although making use of skill*"

Gaudet eques vicisse putans, spernitque bubulcum
    Sudoremque suum tergit ab ore suo.
Ecce moram nescit, equitem speculata morantem
    In cubiti nodum rustica clava ferit.
Huius plaga loci totius corporis aufert
    Robur: cedit eques ipse cadensque sedet.
O nova simplicitas! sedet ipse vocatque sedentem
    Et, nisi surgat eques, surgere velle negat.
"Surge," bubulcus ait. Cui miles: "Surgere nolo."
    Alter ait: "Sedeas, meque sedere licet."

---

aufero, auferre: take, snatch away, remove
bubulcus, -i *m.*: a plowman, farm laborer
cado (3): to fall, drop
cedo (3): to withdraw, concede, submit
clava, -ae *f.*: a club, cudgel
cubitum, -i *n.*: an elbow, forearm
gaudeo (2): to be glad, rejoice
licet (2): to it is permitted (+ *inf.*)
miles, militis *m.*: a soldier, knight
moror (1): to delay
nego (1): to deny, refuse (+ *inf.*)
nescio (4): to not know
nodus, -i *m.*: a knot, node
nolo, nolle: be unwilling to (+ *inf.*)

novus, -a, -um: new, unusual
os, oris *n.*: a face
plaga, -ae *f.*: a stroke, wound
robur, roboris *n.*: strength, military strength
rusticus, -a, -um: rustic
sedeo (2): to sit, remain
simplicitas, simplicitatis *f.*: simplicity
speculor (1): to watch, observe
sperno (3): to scorn, despise, spurn
sudor, sudoris *m.*: sweat
surgo (3): to arise
tergo (3): to rub, wipe, wipe off
voco (1): to call, summon
volo, velle: to wish, want

---

moram nescit: "he doesn't know the delay" i.e. he doesn't realize the strategy
speculata: nom. agreeing with *clava*, "the club, *having observed* the knight" *metonymy*
rustica clava: nom. subj., "*a rustic club* strikes"
sedet ipse: "he himself sits" i.e. the plowman
nisi surgat: pres. subj. in fut. less vivid protasis, "unless the knight were to rise"
surgat ... eat: pres. subj. in ind. com., "orders him *to rise or go* having been defeated"
sedeas: pres. subj. jussive serving as a protasis, "may you sit!" i.e. if you sit

Turba stupet. Praefectus adest equitique moranti

    Imperat aut surgat aut superatus eat.

Haeret eques. Praefectus ait: "Te vicit arator."

    Pugna cadit. Regi panditur ordo rei.

Rex ait: "Incisum noda, praefecte, duellum;

    Dedecus explanet ille vel ille suum."

Pugna redit milesque sedet velut ante sedebat.

    "Surge," bubulcus ait: "Non volo," reddit eques.

Cultor ait: "Dum stare negas ego stare negabo.

    Surgere si temptas, surgere promptus ero."

---

adsum, adesse: to be near
ante: before
cultor, cultoris *m.*: a husbandman
dedecus, dedecoris *n.*: disgrace, shame
eo, ire: to go, walk
explano (1): to make clear
haereo (2): to stick, cling to, hesitate
impero (1): to order, command (+ *dat.*)
incisus, -a, -um: cut short, interrupted
miles, militis *m.*: a soldier, knight
nodo (1): to tie with a knot
ordo, ordinis *m.*: order, series

pando (3): to publish, make known
praefectus, -i *m.*: a commander
promptus, -a -um: ready, eager
pugna, -ae *f.*: a battle, fight
reddo (3): to return
redeo, redire: to return
res, rei *f.*: a thing
stupeo (2): to be astounded
supero (1): to overcome, conquer
tempto (1): to try
turba, -ae *f.*: a crowd, multitude
velut: just as

---

equitique moranti: dat. after *imperat*, "he orders *the delaying knight*"

surgat ... eat: pres. subj. in ind. com., "orders him *to rise ... to go* having been defeated"

regi: dat., "made known *to the king*"

ordo rei: "the order of the matter" i.e. the narrative of the events"

noda: imper., "tie up!" i.e. bring to a conclusion

explanet: pres. subj. jussive, "let that one explain"

ille vel ille: "either that one (the knight) or the other (the plowman)"

pugna redit: "the battle resumes"

surgere: inf. epexegetic with *promptus*, "will be ready *to rise*"

Ambo sedent, ridet populus, praesesque bubulco

Intonat: "Aut pugnes aut fuge. Tempus abit."

Cultor ait: "Surgat! caderet, si surgere vellet."

"Percute," praeses ait: "Percute, surget eques.

Te decet aut illum victi sibi ponere nomen."

"Hoc mihi non ponam nomen," arator ait.

"Surgo, surge, miser! Nam turpe ferire sedentem

Est mihi, sicque tibi turpe sedendo mori."

Sic ait et timidum mulcet; rogat ille furentem:

"Parce precor; vincor, supplico, victor abi."

---

abeo, abire: to depart, go away, pass

cultor, cultoris *m.*: a husbandman, planter

decet (2): to it is fitting, right (+ *acc.* + *inf.*)

fugio (3): to flee, fly

furo (3): to rage

intono (1): to thunder

miser, -a, -um: poor, miserable

morior (3): to die

mulceo (2): to flatter, delight

nomen, nominis *n.*: a name, title

parco (3): to spare, show consideration

percutio (3): to beat, strike

pono (3): to put, place

populus, -i *m.*: a people, nation

praeses, praesidis *m./f.*: a chief, procurator

precor (1): to beg, implore

pugno (1): to fight

rideo (2): to laugh, ridicule

rogo (1): to ask, ask for

supplico (1): to pray, beg

timidus, -a, -um: timid, cowardly

turpis, -e: ugly, shameful

victor, victoris *m.*: a conqueror, victor

---

pugnes: pres. subj. jussive, "may you fight!"

surgat: pres. subj. jussive, "let him rise!"

caderet, si ... vellet: impf. subj. in present contrafactual, "if he were willing, he would die"

victi: perf. part. gen. of specification with *nomen*, "to place the name of 'conquered' to yourself"

ponere: pres. inf. after *decet*, "fitting that either you or that one *place*"

ferire: inf. epex. after *turpe*, "it is foul *to strike*"

Laeta novat fortuna senem; senis unicus haeres

Scribitur et dignas intrat arator opes.

Jus superat vires, sors aspera monstrat amicum.

Plus confert odio gratia, fraude fides.

Fine fruor versu gemino; quod cogitat omnis

Fabula declarat datque quod intus habet.

---

amicus, -i *m.*: a friend
asper, -a, -um: cruel, rough
cogito (1): to reflect on, intend
confero, conferre: to bring together, confer
declaro (1): to declare
dignus, -a, -um: appropriate, worthy
fabula, -ae *f.*: a fable
fides, fidei *f.*: faith, loyalty
finis, finis *m./f.*: an end
fortuna, -ae *f.*: luck, fate
fraus, fraudis *f.*: fraud, trickery
fruor (3): to delight in (+ *abl.*)
geminus, -a, -um: twin, double
gratia, -ae *f.*: favor, goodwill, friendship
habeo (2): to have
heres, heredis *m./f.*: an heir

intro (1): to enter, go into
intus: within
jus, juris *n.*: right, justice
laetus, -a, -um: happy
monstro (1): to show, reveal
novo (1): to refresh, change
odium, -i *n.*: hate, hatred
omnis, omne: each, every
ops, opis *f.*: power, might, wealth
plus: (*adv.*) more
scribo (3): to write, compose
sors, sortis *f.*: lot, fate
supero (1): to overcome
unicus, -a, -um: only, sole, single
versus, -us *m.*: a line, verse
vis, viris *f.*: strength, power

---

sedendo: gerund abl. instrumental, "to die *by sitting*"
odio, fraude: abl. of comp. after *plus*, "more than hatred ... more than fraud"
fine: abl. of place where, "at the end" i.e. the end of each poem
quod cogitat: object of *declarat*, "that which each fable intends"
declarat datque: "(the final couplet) *declares and gives*"
quod intus habet: object of *dat*, "that which each fable has inside"

Glossary

credo (3): to believe, trust in

cum: with (*prep. + abl.*); when, since, although (*conj. + subj.*)

cur: why

A a

a, ab, abs: from, by (+ *abl.*)

abeo, abire: depart, go away, pass

ac: and in addition, and also, and; (+ *comparative*) than

ad: to, up to, towards (+ *acc.*)

ait: he says

ambo, ambae, ambo: both

amicus, -a, -um: friendly

amo (1): to love

amor, amoris *m.*: love

an: or (in questions); utrum … an: whether … or

anguis, anguis *m./f.*: snake

ante: before, in front of (*adv.* and *prep. + acc.*)

arma, -orum *n.*: arms, weapons

ars, artis *f.*: skill

asellus, -i *m.*: small ass, donkey

at: but, moreover, yet

aut: or

avis, avis *f.*: bird

B b

bene: well, very

bibo (3): to drink

bonus, -a, -um: good, noble

bos, bovis *m./f.*: ox, bull, cow

C c

canis, canis *m./f.*: dog; hound

careo (2): to be without; lack

causa, -ae *f.*: cause; reason

caveo (2): to beware, avoid

cibus, -i *m.*: food

cor, cordis *n.*: heart, mind

corpus, corporis *n.*: body; person

D d

de: down from, about, concerning (+ *abl.*)

dens, dentis *m.*: tooth; tusk

dies, diei *m./f.*: day; daylight

diu: (for) a long time

do, dare, dedi, datum: to give

dolor, doloris *m.*: pain, anguish

dum: while (+ *indic.*); until (+ *subj.*); provided that (+ *subj.*)

E e

ecce: behold!

ego, mei, mihi, me: I, me

eo, ire, ivi/ii, itus: to go, walk

equus, -i *m.*: horse; steed

ergo: therefore

et: and

ex, e: out of, from (+ *abl.*)

F f

facio, facere, feci, factum: to do, make

ferio (4): to hit, strike

fero, ferre, tuli, latus: to bear, carry

fio, fiere: to become, happen

fugio (3): to flee, avoid

H h

habeo (2): to have

hic, haec, hoc: this, these

I i

idem, eadem, idem: the same

ille, illa, illud: that

in: in, on (+ *abl.*); into, onto (+ *acc.*)

inde: from there, from then

inquiam, **inquit**: to say (*used with direct speech*)

ipse, **ipsa**, **ipsum**: himself, herself, itself

iste, **ista**, **istud**: that, that of yours

J j

jam, **jamque**: now; already

L l

leo, **leonis** *m.*: a lion

lupus, **-i** *m.*: a wolf

M m

magnus, **-a**, **-um**: large, great

malus, **-a**, **-um**: bad, evil

manus, **manus** *f.*: a hand

mater, **matris** *f.*: a mother

mens, **mentis** *f.*: mind

metus, **-us** *m.*: fear

meus, **-a**, **-um**: my, mine

moveo (2) **movi**, **motus**: to move, provoke

multus, **-a**, **-um**: much, many

munus, **muneris** *n.*: a duty, gift

mus, **muris** *m./f.*: a mouse

N n

nam, **namque**: for, indeed, really

ne: lest, that not (+ *subj.*)

nec: and not, nor; **nec...nec**: neither...nor

nego (1): to deny

nil: nothing

nisi, **ni**: if not, unless

noceo (2) **nocui**: harm, hurt

non: not

nos, **nostrum/nostri**, **nobis**, **nos**: we

nullus, **-a**, **-um**: not any, no one

nunc: now

O o

ob: against, on account of (+ *acc.*)

omnis, **omne**: every, all

ops, **opis** *f.*: power, assistance, resources, wealth

os, **oris** *n.*: a mouth, face

ovis, **ovis** *f.*: a sheep

P p

per: through (+ *acc.*)

pereo (4): to be destroyed; go to waste

pes, **pedis** *m.*: a foot

peto (3): to seek, attack

placeo (2): to please, satisfy

plus: (*adv.*) more

poena, **-ae** *f.*: a penalty, punishment

possum, **posse**, **potui**, -: to be able, be possible

premo (3) **pressi**, **pressus**: to press, strike

pro: for, on behalf of, in proportion to (+ *abl.*)

prosum, **prodesse**: to be useful, benefit

puto (1): to think, believe

Q q

quam: how?; (*after comparative*) than

-que: (*enclitic*) and

qui, **quae**, **quod**: who, which, what

quis, **quid**: who? what? which?

R r

rana, **-ae** *f.*: a frog

rapio (3) **rapui**, **raptus**: to snatch, seize

reddo (3): to return

redeo, **redire**, **redii**, **reditus**: to return

res, **rei** *f.*: a thing

rex, **regis** *m.*: a king

S s

saepe: often

sed: but

senex, senis (*gen.*): aged, old

sequor (3), **secutus sum**: to follow

seu: or if, whether

si: if

sic: in this manner, thus; **sic ... ut**: in the same way as

sine: without

solus, -a, -um: only, alone

spes, spei *f.*: hope

sto (1), **steti, status**: to stand

sub: under, near (+ *acc.* and *abl.*)

sui, sibi, se/sese: him/her/itself, themselves

sum, esse, fui, futurus: to be, exist

suus, sua, suum: his/her/its (own), (*pl.*) their (own)

T t

tamen: nevertheless, still

tantus, -a, -um: of such size; so great

tempus, temporis *n.*: time

timeo (2): to fear, dread, be afraid

timor, timoris *m.*: fear; dread

tu, tui, tibi, te: you (*sing.*)

tutus, -a, -um: safe, secure

U u

ubi: where, when

unus, -a, -um: one

ut, uti: as (+ indic.); so that, with the result that (+ subj.)

V v

vel: or else, or; even; **vel ... vel**: either ... or

verbum, -i *n.*: a word

video (2), **vidi, visus**: see

vir, -i *m.*: man

vis, viris *f.*: strength

vita, -ae *f.*: life

vivo (3), **vixi, victus**: to live

vix: hardly, scarcely

volo, velle, volui: to wish, want

vulnus, vulneris *n.*: a wound

vulpes, vulpis *f.*: a fox

NOTES:

NOTES:

NOTES:

NOTES:

NOTES:

NOTES:

NOTES:

NOTES:

NOTES:

NOTES:

Made in the USA
Lexington, KY
09 July 2019